Soul Communication
Opening Your Spiritual Channels
for Success and Fulfillment

Heaven's Library

by Master Zhi Gang Sha

Typeset in Cochin

Printed in USA

First Edition

10 9 8 7 6 5 4 3 2 1

Heaven's Library
Soul Wisdom Series

The purpose of life is to serve. I am a universal servant. You are a universal servant. Everyone and everything is a universal servant. A universal servant offers universal service, including universal love, forgiveness, peace, healing, blessing, harmony and enlightenment.

My total life mission is to transform the consciousness of humanity and souls in the universe, in order to join all souls as one to create a peaceful and harmonized world and universe. This mission includes three empowerments.

My first empowerment is to teach universal service, empowering people to be unconditional universal servants. The message of universal service is:

I am a universal servant.

You are a universal servant.

Everyone and everything is a universal servant.

A universal servant offers universal service unconditionally, including universal love, forgiveness, peace, healing, blessing, harmony and enlightenment.

I serve humanity and the universe unconditionally.

You serve humanity and the universe unconditionally.

Together, we serve humanity and the universe unconditionally.

My second life mission is to teach healing, empowering people to heal themselves and others. The message of healing is:

I have the power to heal myself.

You have the power to heal yourself.

Together, we have the power to heal the world.

My third life mission is to teach soul wisdom, empowering people to transform their lives and enlighten their souls, minds and bodies. The message of soul wisdom is:

I have the power to transform my life and enlighten my soul, mind and body.

You have the power to transform your life and enlighten your soul, mind and body.

Together, we have the power to transform the world and enlighten humanity and all souls.

The beginning of the twenty-first century is Mother Earth's transition period into the Soul Light Era. Natural disasters, tsunamis, hurricanes, earthquakes, floods, drought, extreme temperatures, famine, disease, political and religious wars, terrorism and other such upheavals are part of this transition. Millions of people on Mother Earth are suffering from depression, anxiety, fear, anger and worry. They suffer from pain, chronic conditions and life-threatening illnesses. Humanity needs help. The consciousness of humanity needs to be transformed. The suffering of humanity needs to be removed.

One of the most pressing needs of humanity and all souls at this time is access to divine wisdom and its gifts of knowledge, insight, love, forgiveness, compassion and peace. Sacred writings have been made available throughout history to pass down heavenly wisdom and knowledge to those who are open to receiving and disseminating it. In past ages, however, the true writings, true wisdom and true sacred knowledge were distorted or diluted to suit the purposes of the cultures, political structures and religious institutions of the time.

Now, much sacred knowledge is flowing to Mother Earth to help raise the consciousness of humanity and all souls. At this historic period, Heaven's Library has been formed under Divine Guidance to assist in this mission. The objective of Heaven's Library is to

offer a series of divine teachings on soul wisdom that reveal soul secrets and practical tools and treasures to empower people to heal and
enlighten themselves and others, to transform every aspect of life,
and to create a harmonized and enlightened world and universe.

In 2003, I was chosen as a divine servant, vehicle and channel to
transmit permanent divine healing and blessing treasures to humanity and souls in the universe. These healings and blessings can be
physical, emotional, mental or spiritual, and they cover all aspects of
life, including relationships and finances.

The Divine has guided me to transmit particular abilities to selected individuals in order to create Divine Writers for Heaven's
Library. They are also called Divine Writing Channels of Zhi Gang
Sha. Each is assigned a series of Heaven's Library books to flow in
my voice. The titles come from the Divine. Each series and each title
is tailor-made for this representative of humanity at this particular
time in his or her soul journey. The content also comes from the
Divine. The books cover many aspects of life — ancient wisdom, in-
digenous wisdom, guidance on the life stages of babies, adolescents
and adults, various professions, parenting, music, yoga, business,
education, technology and more. Their primary focus is to deliver
soul wisdom, which includes divine love, forgiveness, compassion,
intelligence, knowledge and practice on all of these topics.

I have transmitted permanent divine treasures to the Divine
Writers to open their divine writing channel and to download the
divine books to their souls. Then, after invoking these gifts as they
sit to write, they deliver my books by flow. This means the Divine
Writing Channels "borrow the mouth and hands" to flow and write
out these divine teachings on every aspect of life. They do not use
their "logical heads" to think about how to write or what to write.
Instead, they call upon the gifts and then write down what they in-
wardly hear. We also have Divine Editors who have received spe-
cialized permanent divine downloads to edit these books. I do a final

review and approval. This is how the divine books in Heaven's Library are produced.

The Soul Wisdom Series books produced by Heaven's Library are totally committed universal servants. Open your heart and soul to read these books. Apply the wisdom, knowledge and practice in these books to heal, transform and enlighten your life. Heaven's Library is very honored to announce to all humanity and to all souls in the universe that divine teaching, including divine wisdom, knowledge and practice in every aspect of life, will be revealed and shared in its publications.

Digest it. Absorb it. Apply it. Benefit from it.

I love my heart and soul.

I love all humanity.

Join hearts and souls together.

Love, peace and harmony.

Love, peace and harmony.

These divine teachings will serve you always.

With love and blessing,

Master Zhi Gang Sha

Soul Communication

CONTENTS

Introduction

There are thousands, even millions, of people worldwide who want to do soul communication. Their souls have yearned for this for many years. Some have waited for many lifetimes. Most likely, you are one of these people. All of you now have the opportunity to learn how to do soul communication.

Soul communication is a profound gift for this era, the Soul Light Era which began on August 8, 2003. I will have more to say about the Soul Light Era later in this book. Soul communication makes it possible to have a direct conversation with the Divine, with the highest saints, with any soul you wish to communicate with. The wisdom, healing, rejuvenation and transformation that come from soul communication are without limits. You will be amazed at how soul communication will change your life. Many secrets will be revealed to you. The root of some obstacles will be revealed. Health issues, including illness and aging, will be helped. I do not promise anything, but know that using the teachings in this book will be life-transforming.

Soul communication is a key to priceless treasures. These treasures include opening your spiritual channels, receiving teachings from the highest levels of the Soul World, being in the presence of an extraordinary frequency connected with the topic of your communication, and much, much more. You will learn about these treasures in this book.

This book also includes many practical suggestions and simple practices. Some of these may be familiar to you. Everything may be completely new to you. It doesn't matter. Use this book to understand soul communication as the treasure it is. Use this book to learn how to do soul communication. Use this book to learn how to apply soul communication to benefit every aspect of your life. Use this book to help you open your spiritual channels. Use this book to receive blessings, because every aspect of this book is a blessing to those who use it.

The more blessings you receive, the higher your frequency will be. This is very important, because high-level teachings are given only to those who can handle them. If your frequency is low, the wisdom you receive will be limited. All of this can change by using this book to receive the blessings you need. These blessings will assist you in making every teaching in this book part of your life. This book is a healing and blessing tool to serve you.

It is my honor and privilege to offer these teachings to humanity at this critical time of transition for humanity and Mother Earth. It is also my honor and privilege to share the wisdom and insights so that you can experience their power and benefits. I am profoundly grateful to my most beloved spiritual father and adoptive father, Master Zhi Chen Guo, for opening the gate to this information for me. Without his teachings, I would never have been able to write this book. He has generously shared many secrets and much wisdom with me. It is my honor and privilege to offer these teachings to you, to all humanity and beyond.

Thank you. Thank you. Thank you.

Master Zhi Gang Sha

What is Soul Communication?

Communication is one of the most important aspects of life, not only human life but all life. In your life, you communicate with your family members. You communicate with your colleagues. You communicate with your friends. In our modern world, we communicate using telephones and the Internet, through radio and television and via satellites. With advanced technology, scientists communicate with our cells and cell units, and with planets, stars and galaxies. Communication is a vital part of everyone's life.

Communication is taking place constantly on Mother Earth, all around us as well as within us. We use countless ways to communicate in our lives. Communication takes place not only among human beings, but also among animals, plants and insects. Think of the language and intelligence of dolphins, the migration of birds and the organization of a beehive. Think of how plants respond to the beautiful melodies and harmonies of Mozart. Think of how the DNA and RNA in your cells communicate across generations. All animate things communicate.

Did you know that inanimate objects communicate also? Everything in the room in which you are reading this book communicates. The company you work for communicates. The car you drive communicates. Mountains and rivers communicate. Mother Earth communicates. They all communicate with each other. This book is communicating with you now.

You can communicate with all animate and inanimate things. You can communicate with "things" that do not have physical form, which are in the spiritual realms or, as I call it, the Soul World. You can do this using soul communication. Through soul communication, you can receive wisdom, knowledge and healing from any soul in the universe. This book will teach you how.

Everything has a soul. A human being has a soul. An animal has a soul. A plant has a soul. A flower has a soul. A mountain has a soul. A river has a soul. Does a soul communicate with other souls? How does a soul communicate? What is the significance of doing soul communication? What are its benefits? How can you open your spiritual channels to do soul communication? I am delighted to reveal the soul wisdom and soul secrets of soul communication to you. This book will answer all of these questions and much more.

Soul communication is communication between soul and soul. Soul communication is also communication between soul and mind. Why do we need soul communication? We need it because we want to understand our soul's desires and purpose. You have no doubt thought about the purpose of your life. Does a soul have a life purpose? The answer is clear. Yes! A soul has a clear life purpose. Your soul has its life purpose. Every human being's soul has its life purpose. An animal's soul also has its life purpose. Does a plant's or a mountain's soul have a purpose for its life? The answer is clear. Yes! Every soul has a purpose for its own life.

What is the purpose of a soul's life? *Every soul's purpose is to uplift its soul standing.* What is soul standing? Let me reveal the soul secrets about soul standing. As human beings, we are in the realm of the universe which has nine layers or levels of souls. The lowest layer is the ninth one, Level 9. The highest layer is Level 1.

A newborn soul comes to Mother Earth and floats in nature. It may attach to a rock, a flower or a tree. It experiences physical life. These souls are in Level 9. Through many lifetimes, these souls learn and grow through their own experiences. They are then ready to become a Level 8 or Level 7 soul, which can be the soul of a mountain, a river or a forest. At these levels, souls continue to learn from their life experiences and offer service to nature and society. The soul will advance to higher layers and reincarnate as an animal. The souls of animals stand on Level 6 or Level 5. These souls continue to serve the universe. They continue to learn their lessons. They continue to improve themselves. As they do all of this, they continue to increase their spiritual standing. When they have done a good job, these animal souls are uplifted to the human being's layer. The soul standing of human beings is Level 4 or Level 3. Human beings uplift their spiritual standing by offering good service, including unconditional love, forgiveness, kindness, compassion, integrity, generosity and more. When human beings have done an exceptionally good job, the spiritual world will uplift their souls to the saint level. These souls become holy saints, buddhas, Taoist saints, ascended masters, archangels, major gurus or major lamas. The spiritual standing of these beings is Level 2 or Level 1.

Each step in the soul's journey from Level 9 to Level 1 could take hundreds of lifetimes. This teaching on soul standing in the universe has been the insight received by my spiritual father, Master Zhi Chen Guo, and me. We are honored to reveal these secrets. You may or may not agree with our teaching. It is our personal insight and understanding. We honor your insight and perspective. Because Master Guo and I are universal servants, we simply share what we know. We are honored to have the opportunity to serve.

Why do I reveal these soul secrets? I share these secrets so that you can understand the purpose of your soul and of every soul. Now that you know about the layers of soul standing, you may ask, "Why should I care about increasing my soul standing?" Think about history. How many holy saints, healing angels, archangels, ascended masters, buddhas, Taoist saints, lamas and Indian gurus have served humanity and Mother Earth? Why do they serve unconditionally? Their purpose is in alignment with their souls' purpose: to uplift their soul standing.

A high-level soul has high wisdom, intelligence, knowledge and abilities to serve. Millions of people know the stories of the Bible. Millions of people know the stories of Buddha. Why are these stories so powerful? They are powerful because the power is given by the Divine and the universe. This power is soul power or spiritual power. It is not any other kind of power.

Every soul in the universe desires to uplift its spiritual standing to be closer to the Divine. Spiritual law states that the higher your spiritual standing, the greater the soul power given to you by the Divine. A soul does not wish to increase its standing to satisfy its ego. It wants to increase its standing to gain abilities to serve humanity, Mother Earth and the universe.

To be closer to the Divine, you must be more like the Divine. There is only one way to uplift your soul standing: offer unconditional universal service. Universal service includes universal love, forgiveness, peace, healing, blessing, harmony and enlightenment. If you offer a little service, you receive a little blessing from the Divine and the universe. If you offer more service, you receive more blessings. If you offer unconditional universal service, you receive unlimited blessings.

At this time, let us join hearts and souls in a simple practice to offer unconditional service to all of humanity and all souls in the universe. Let us offer service to uplift every soul. We can do this by chanting the mantra Unconditional Universal Service repeatedly. Say:

Dear soul, mind and body of Unconditional Universal Service, I love you. Can you please offer service to all humanity and all souls in the universe? Uplift their hearts and souls. I am honored and blessed. I cannot thank you enough. Thank you. Thank you. Thank you.

Then, chant *unconditional universal service, unconditional universal service, unconditional universal service, unconditional universal service.* Chant repeatedly for at least three minutes, the longer the better. The more you offer service, the more virtue you will gain and the more you will uplift your soul standing. Your life will be blessed tremendously by offering service in this way. The mantra Unconditional Universal Service connects you to the Divine and to all souls so that you can offer your total love, forgiveness, care and compassion. This practical treasure can be applied at any time, anywhere, silently or out loud. The only requirement is for you to be sincere and have an open heart.

❄ ❄ ❄ ❄

The soul's journey depends on reincarnation. I personally believe deeply in reincarnation. Reincarnation is one of the most important spiritual laws. We are in the realm of Jiu Tian, the nine layers of Heaven that I briefly explained above. All souls in Jiu Tian reincarnate from lifetime to lifetime as they uplift their soul standing with the goal of reaching Level 1. But Level 1 souls, which are a very high saint level, continue to move their soul standing further. The next step for Level 1 souls is to be uplifted to a realm beyond the nine layers of Heaven. That realm is named Tian Wai Tian, which literally means the "Heaven beyond Heaven." If a Level 1 soul has served humanity, Mother Earth and the universe very well, Heaven and the Divine can decide to uplift that Level 1 soul to Tian Wai Tian.

What is the most significant aspect of being uplifted to Tian Wai Tian? *Reincarnation stops for a soul in Tian Wai Tian.* That soul will stay in Tian Wai Tian, which is within the divine realm. That soul will not reincarnate as a human being any more. That soul will stay in the

Soul World forever. That soul will continue to serve humanity and the universe in a special way, because a soul in Tian Wai Tian has much more powerful abilities to serve than a soul in Jiu Tian.

These are the basic soul secrets about soul standing in Jiu Tian and the possibility of being uplifted to Tian Wai Tian. This is the soul's purpose for all souls in the universe. How can you know where your soul stands? Soul communication is the treasure which can give you the answer to this question and many other questions about your soul journey.

Soul communication is vital spiritual wisdom for understanding your spiritual journey. It can tell you what your current spiritual standing is. It can tell you about your journey through your past lives, the condition of your soul journey in your present life, and the prospects for your soul journey in your future lives. Physical life is very short. Spiritual life is eternal. The purpose of physical life is to serve spiritual life. Soul communication will guide your physical journey so that you can accomplish your spiritual journey.

Through soul communication, you can receive direct guidance from the Divine. Anyone can learn how to communicate directly with the Divine and the highest spiritual teachers in Heaven. Open your soul communication channels to directly receive their teaching, wisdom and knowledge. This will increase your intelligence and your abilities to benefit every aspect of your life.

Through soul communication, you can also directly invoke the Divine and high spiritual beings to request their healing and blessings for your life, including your relationships and business. Open your soul communication channels to allow soul communication to transform every aspect of your life. Transformation can be applied to businesses, careers, relationships, emotions, physical conditions and your entire spiritual journey. You can use soul communication for all aspects of your life. The only limitation is your own flexibility and creativity. The possibilities for transformation are limitless.

I have taught hundreds of students worldwide to open their spiritual channels. These students have opened their spiritual channels by communicating with the Divine daily and by receiving blessings to purify and transform their spiritual channels. Furthermore, I have created about one hundred Divine Writers who have opened their divine writing channels. The Divine Writers receive wisdom and teaching directly from the spiritual world to empower every aspect of life. You can receive all of the benefits that they have received and are receiving.

Many people have had the desire to communicate with the Divine, the highest saints and all aspects of the Soul World. It is entirely possible to do this. It is my desire to teach thousands, even millions of people to do this. I am committed to teach soul communication to humanity. Reading and using this book is one way to develop your soul communication abilities. Humanity is waiting for the opportunity to have soul communication be part of daily life. As more and more people do soul communication, blessings and healings will touch every part of daily life.

Soul communication is not limited to those on a spiritual journey. It is open to all humanity. Imagine how different Mother Earth will be as more and more people develop their ability to do soul communication. It is a gift to each individual. It is also a gift to all humanity and to Mother Earth.

Allow me to be your servant by sharing soul wisdom and soul secrets about soul communication. Allow me to share secret techniques to open your spiritual channels. Allow me to serve you by sharing the soul wisdom to facilitate your spiritual journey. Soul communication will serve you well if you are willing to uplift your spiritual standing and fulfill your spiritual journey. It will serve you well if you are willing to transform every aspect of your life.

Your soul has been waiting for this message. It is happy this opportunity is available. You will receive powerful teachings and blessings to develop your soul communication ability as you read this book. Receive the blessings. Learn the wisdom. Put it into practice. Benefit from it.

Significance of Soul Communication

Why does your soul want to do soul communication? It is very simple. Your soul wants to serve. It wants to accelerate its journey. It wants greater participation in divine light, love, forgiveness and every other divine quality. It wants to have access to the secrets of the universe. When you use soul communication, all of this is available to you.

I'm delighted to share a vital wisdom for the soul journey. A soul has many lifetimes. In every lifetime, a soul serves family, society and humanity. The activities, behaviors and thoughts of the soul are recorded in Heaven, in a place named the Akashic Records.[1] If a soul offers good service, including love, care, compassion, sincerity, generosity, kindness, integrity and purity in one lifetime, that soul will uplift its spiritual standing in that life. If a soul offers unpleasant service, such as killing, harming, cheating or stealing, that soul's spiritual standing will drop.

Your soul has had many lifetimes. In some lifetimes its standing increased. In other lifetimes it dropped. Your soul has been on a journey where its level has gone up and down many times. Throughout this journey, it has wanted a way to keep itself on the right path to avoid getting lost. Soul communication can tell you about the soul journey of your previous lives, current life and future lives. It will give you clear direction to advance your soul journey.

Your soul has many qualities and characteristics. One of those is the desire to learn. There are many reasons your soul wants to learn. The most important one is to stay on the path to light. It wants to know how to do this in a better way. Your soul has great wisdom that it has acquired during its many lifetimes. It has much good karma, which is good virtue. All of this has helped your soul on its journey by keeping the goals of the journey in your soul's awareness. All of this has helped keep your soul on the proper path.

However, this is not the whole story. What about the times when your soul forgot about its proper journey? In some lifetimes, you made mistakes. You did things that resulted in bad karma and the loss of good virtue. All of these mistakes, whether actions, behaviors or attitudes, result in lessons. The more serious the mistakes, the more serious the lessons. Your soul knows this. It knows it has many lessons to learn.

Even if you are karma-free, there are still lessons to learn. There are soul memories to heal. Your soul is very aware of this. Learning its lessons is important to your soul. Your soul can learn these lessons the hard way, through trial and error, or your soul can learn the lessons more directly and more efficiently. This does not mean there will be no suffering, or that it will be easy. Even when the lessons are learned in a direct way, there will be struggle involved in releasing behaviors and attitudes. Behaviors and attitudes are two of the most evident ways in which the lessons your soul has carried from previous lifetimes are made present in this lifetime. Releasing and transforming behaviors and attitudes can be difficult.

Your behaviors and attitudes are connected to many mindsets, beliefs and attachments. These behaviors and attitudes are actually gifts to you. They let you know what lessons you need to learn. They let you know what mindsets, beliefs and attachments you need to release. When you do the releasing and learn the lessons, your related karma is transformed to light. This is a priceless treasure and gift for your soul. It accelerates your soul journey more than you can imagine. Transforming the karma connected to your behaviors and attitudes almost always means that you are free and clear of that karma. You have learned the lessons. There is no need for you to learn the lessons again.

Even after you learn the lessons and transform your karma, you may still need to review the lessons. You also need to practice your new, transformed behaviors and attitudes. However, this is much easier than learning the lessons for the first time. It is like driving a car. Once you learn how to drive, you have that skill for life. You learned the skill, took a test and received your driver's license. However, to become a really good driver, you need experience. You need to continue to practice. When lessons are learned and karma is transformed, it is similar. To totally transform yourself to new behaviors and attitudes, you must put them into practice.

Forgiveness is the key to cleansing karma. It brings the quality of divine peace into all aspects of your life, including relationships, health, business and finances. You can offer forgiveness to all the souls that you have hurt. Also, you can forgive all the souls that have hurt you. If you offer forgiveness unconditionally, your life will be blessed. You can use a Universal Meditation discussed in my book *Soul Mind Body Medicine*[2] to offer forgiveness to cleanse your karma.

Say: *Dear soul, mind and body of all the souls that I have hurt, can you please sit in my lower abdomen? Can you please forgive me? I am sincerely sorry, from the bottom of my heart. I offer you my total love. I cannot thank you enough.*

Then, do not forget to invite all the souls that have hurt you and offer them forgiveness. Say: *Dear soul, mind and body of all the souls that have hurt me, I love you all. Can you please sit in my lower abdomen? I forgive you for any harm that you may have caused me. I offer you love and blessings. I deeply appreciate and honor you. Thank you.*

Next, chant *unconditional forgiveness, unconditional forgiveness, unconditional forgiveness, unconditional forgiveness* repeatedly, for at least three minutes, the longer the better.

Do this exercise daily to offer unconditional forgiveness. Some souls will forgive you the first time you do this exercise. Some will not. The more you offer your unconditional forgiveness, more and more souls will forgive you. This practical exercise will bring profound transformation to all aspects of your life.

In addition to transforming karma, your soul wants to heal its memories. These memories are also evident in your present life. They can also be observed in your behaviors and attitudes. How can behaviors and attitudes be the result of soul memories? Let me give you an example. If you were a powerful teacher of wisdom in a previous lifetime, in this lifetime you will be a powerful student of wisdom. You may also again be a powerful teacher of wisdom. Your soul remembers this past lifetime. Your soul remembers all of its past lifetimes. These soul memories become present in this lifetime. For example, if in past lifetimes you did not complete some of your spiritual tasks, in this lifetime you may have resistance to similar spiritual tasks and roles. On the other hand, it is possible that you will be attracted to certain roles because your soul wants to complete its tasks. Your soul knows the importance of completing its spiritual tasks. These examples give you an idea of how soul memories are present in this lifetime.

These teachings are a basis for appreciating the significance of soul communication. Using soul communication, you can make a direct connection with a past life. You can connect with your resistance in this life and ask what its lesson is. You can request a blessing to release your resistance. This example of doing soul communication with your resistance is useful because resistance is a common experience. Through soul communication, you can ask, "What is the source of my resistance? What is its root?" When you communicate soul to soul, you receive an instantaneous answer and, in most cases, the answer is accurate.[3]

One treasure of soul communication is its ability to go directly to the essence of a situation, question or problem. You can receive information about the root of the issue. You can receive a teaching on how to resolve the issue. All of this can happen in as little as one minute, although you can also spend much more time in soul communication if that is appropriate for your particular issue. This is very different from using logical thinking. Logical thinking is still important and necessary. It is integral to all aspects of our life. However, when it comes to the soul journey, it is not enough. Using logical thinking, it is very rare for anyone to get an answer to a dilemma in one minute. People spend hours, days and even weeks or months struggling with how to change a particular behavior or attitude when they use logical thinking. What a great gift it is to have soul communication as a possibility. To be able to get an answer in one minute, in ten minutes, or even in an hour is much easier than struggling to get an answer over weeks or even months. This one aspect alone of soul communication tells you what a wonderful treasure soul communication is. It tells you how significant it is to your soul journey. It tells you why your soul has wanted you to have the ability to do soul communication and to develop this ability to its highest potential.

Soul communication transforms your entire life. You receive teachings, wisdom and healing. Soul communication changes your frequency. This makes it possible for you to connect with higher levels of the Soul World. You can receive profound teachings. These teachings and wisdom will become part of your daily life. You will notice yourself saying things that surprise you. You will wonder where they came from. People will tell you how helpful your remarks are. This is part of the significance of soul communication. When you are connected soul to soul, the messages and the information become part of your being. Your mind might not be aware of this, but your soul knows it.

What you receive in soul communication becomes part of your soul journey. You will experience making surprising comments again and again. This experience will become part of your daily life. This is a great blessing. Every time you use a teaching you have received, you receive a blessing from that teaching. Everyone with whom you share the teaching receives a blessing.

If you are a school teacher, for example, you will notice that you speak differently to your students. You will be able to give very powerful answers to your students' questions, because your answers will be influenced by the wisdom and blessing of your soul communication. Your students will benefit greatly. They will learn better because they will be taught with a direct connection to the Soul World. This does not mean that you will be teaching them about soul communication. It means that everything you do and say will benefit from the soul communication you have done. There will be greater wisdom in your answers. This is true whether the subject is science, art, history or typing. The subject of the class is not relevant. The fact that you are doing soul communication is important. The wisdom your soul has gained becomes part of everything you say and do. You are being transformed on every level: soul, mind, emotion and body.

Pay attention to these changes. Recording them gives you a measure of the transformation taking place. When you look back at notes you made one month ago, three months ago and six months ago, you will notice great changes. Having this kind of record is very helpful in your soul journey. You will share some of your story with others because sharing your story is great service. You will not share your entire story, but only what is appropriate at the time. The benefits will be great. Sharing your story gives others clarity and encouragement. It gives others a model for what they are trying to learn. It helps others know that they are not the first to deal with a particular experience or issue and, more than likely, will not be the last.

Stories are powerful teachers. They carry the message. They also carry the particular gifts, abilities and wisdom of the soul sharing the story. It is not enough to have one or two people share their stories. Hundreds, thousands, even more must share their stories. This is important because no two people connect in exactly the same way with any one story. The more stories there are, the more people will feel that they are included, important and valued.

Sharing stories is a powerful way to teach. It is also a very easy and enjoyable way to teach. When someone comes to you with a question, concern or issue, you could have a lengthy conversation. Or, you could listen with your heart and then share an experience or story that connects with the other person's heart. When this happens, the other person knows he has been heard. Knowing that one has been heard is very healing. It can open the door to a greater participation in divine light and love.

Every time you share your story, those around you are blessed and healed. They receive wonderful wisdom teachings. You are also blessed. The Akashic Records write in your book in gold every time you share. To realize that you can gain huge amounts of virtue simply by sharing your story is extraordinary.

When I talk about sharing your story, I am speaking specifically of sharing about your soul journey. Sharing other aspects of your story can also be helpful and healing. However, it is the story of your soul journey that is truly significant. It is this story that is transforming. Through soul communication, you are directed as to what to share, how to share it and with whom you can share it. Not every part of your story can be shared equally. Some people would not understand some of your experiences, such as some of your soul communication, and it could actually be harmful to them.

If you are not certain about sharing, simply ask your soul. (I will teach you how to do this in the next chapter.) The first response you receive will be the most accurate. Do not try to second-guess your response. Do not analyze it. Your response will make sense. Logical thinking has its place, but in this situation, it is not needed or helpful.

There are many aspects to soul communication. It involves much more than sitting down quietly and meditating. That is a very important and sacred activity, but it does not give a complete picture of soul communication. At certain times of the day, you will sit quietly and record what you receive. You may use a tape recorder. You may use your computer. You may write everything out by hand. How you record your communication is your choice. It is only a tool for you. The important thing is for you to do soul communication.

I suggest that you set aside a time at the beginning of your day for soul communication. If you prefer, you may end your day doing soul communication. Commit a time to the practice of soul communication. However, your soul communication should not be limited to this time. As you read this book, you will appreciate that soul communication is done throughout your day. It does not always have to be your sole focus. Soul communication can happen as you are having a conversation with a friend. It can happen as you are driving your car, washing the dishes or sweeping the floor. There are no limits to the possibilities of making soul-to-soul connections. In fact, your entire day can be lived as a continuous connection with the Soul World. This is a great blessing of healing, rejuvenation and transformation. It is a very high level of service.

Later in this book, I will explain the special connection that soul communication gives us with the Divine, the highest saints and all souls. I have used the term "all souls" many times. In my teachings, everything has a soul. You have a soul. Your heart has a soul. Every organ has a soul. Every system, every cell, every strand of DNA and RNA in your body has a soul. The chair you are sitting on and the floor beneath you have souls. Everything that surrounds you has a soul. The calendar hanging on the wall, a bar of soap, the plants in and around your home, this book — everything has a soul. Keep this in your awareness. Your response to life will be on a completely different level.

Everything has a soul. We are honored and privileged to communicate with all of these souls.

Opening Your Communication Channels

To receive soul communication, you must open your soul, or spiritual, communication channels. These channels include your Third Eye and your Message Center. The Third Eye receives images from the Soul World. The Message Center often receives messages in audible form. Many people whose Message Center is widely open can actually hear messages sent from the Soul World. I will offer more complete teachings on each of these ways of receiving soul communication in Chapter 2.

The primary entry point for all of the soul communication channels is the Message Center, which is also known as the heart chakra. It is in the middle of the chest between the nipples and about two-and-a-half *cun* inside the body.[4] The Message Center is roughly the size of your fist. It has an entry point in the front of your body, on the chest. There are also two entry points in your back between the shoulder blades on either side of the spine. Some people receive messages directly through the crown chakra on the top of the head. The primary pathway of the communication channel is between the Message Center and the crown chakra.

Because messages can come to the Message Center through the entry points between your shoulder blades, many people on the spiritual journey experience tightness or pain in this part of the back. This indicates the need for a more fully open Message Center. As you begin to open your Message Center, this area might become more uncomfortable. That is a blessing. It means that your Message

Center is opening. Blockages are being cleared and light is circulating more freely. These are all gifts from the Divine. These are all very special blessings. The appropriate response is "thank you."

Sometimes people have difficulty saying "thank you" when they are experiencing pain. People say it is hard to be thankful for the pain. The gratitude is not for the pain; it is for the blessing. The pain lets you know that you are receiving the blessing. It lets you know that a great deal of purification is taking place. These are the reasons to say "thank you."

All soul communication channels need to be grounded in a very strong and solid Lower Dan Tian and Snow Mountain Area. If these two foundational energy centers are not strong, you will become drained by soul communication. You could even get sick. If you want to have a high-quality Message Center and Third Eye, you must have a fully developed Lower Dan Tian and Snow Mountain Area.

It is not difficult to develop a strong Lower Dan Tian and Snow Mountain Area. Do not skip the teaching that follows on how to do this. You may be tempted to jump to the sections on opening the Message Center and developing the Third Eye. Do not do that. You will slow your progress on your spiritual journey. You will limit the accuracy of the messages you receive. You will limit the images you can receive from the Soul World through your Third Eye. Be patient. Allow your soul communication channels to open step by step. Build your foundation first.

Home builders know a solid foundation is essential. If a house is going to stand firm through storms and earthquakes, it must have a strong foundation. This is also true for your soul communication channels. If your communication channels are going to be strong, they have to have a solid foundation. If they are going to be solid through times of heavy use, the foundation must be there. If they are going to be solid during times of spiritual testing, the foundation must be there. It must be strong. I cannot tell you enough how important this is. Even though I am emphasizing the importance of the two foundational energy centers, you may still be tempted to skip these pages and go directly to the sections on opening the communication channels. This would be a big mistake!

Developing the Lower Dan Tian

The Lower Dan Tian energy center is located in the lower abdomen. It is centered 1.5 *cun* below the navel and 2.5 *cun* inside the body. This fist-sized energy center is a key for stamina, vitality, immunity and long life. There are many techniques to develop the Lower Dan Tian. Here is a basic approach. Sit on a cushion in a full lotus, half-lotus or simply cross your legs. You may also sit in a chair. Be sure to keep your feet flat on the floor and your back free. You may also stand with your feet shoulder-width apart. Place the tip of your tongue so that it is almost touching the roof of your mouth. Put your hands in the Yin/Yang Palm position. To do this, wrap your right hand around your outstretched left thumb. Then, wrap your left hand over the fingers of your right hand. Squeeze your left thumb with your right hand using about eighty percent of your maximum strength, keeping the rest of your body relaxed. Place your Yin/Yang Palm over your Lower Dan Tian.[5]

Next, say *hello*[6] as follows: *Dear soul, mind and body of my Lower Dan Tian, I love you. You have the power to boost yourself. Boost your energy and power. Develop the highest quality. Do a good job. Thank you.* This is Soul Power, one of the Four Power Techniques of Soul Mind Body Medicine.

Now, visualize golden light coming from all directions to your Lower Dan Tian. Picture all of this light condensing into a very bright golden ball of light in your Lower Dan Tian, brighter than the sun. If you cannot see this, then simply imagine it. This is Mind Power.

For Sound Power, you can chant *light* or *jiu* (the number 9 in Chinese, pronounced "joe").[7] Do this practice three to five times per day, three to five minutes per time. If you can practice for longer, say fifteen minutes or more, even better. Always close your practice with gratitude: *Thank you. Thank you. Thank you.*

My book *Soul Mind Body Medicine* presents other techniques for building the Lower Dan Tian. For example, you can use Universal Meditation. However, it is always helpful to do a standing practice. This will accelerate the development of your Lower Dan Tian.

Developing the Snow Mountain Area

Visualize a line going from your navel straight back to your back. From your back, go forward along this line one-third of the way in. From this point, go down two-and-a-half *cun*. The Snow Mountain Area is centered here. It is a fist-sized energy center also known as the kundalini.

Your Snow Mountain Area also needs to be strong. To develop your Snow Mountain Area, place your Yin/Yang Palm on your lower back, slightly above your tailbone. Say *hello: Dear soul, mind and body of my Snow Mountain Area, I love you. You have the power to build your strength and develop the highest quality. Do a good job. Thank you.*

Now, visualize golden, rainbow, purple or crystal light coming from all directions to your Snow Mountain Area. Picture all of this light condensing into a very bright ball of light in your Snow Mountain Area, brighter than the sun. For Sound Power, you can chant *light* or *jiu* (the number 9 in Chinese, pronounced "joe").

Do this practice three to five times per day, three to five minutes per time. If you can practice for longer, say twenty minutes or more, even better. Close with gratitude: *Thank you. Thank you. Thank you.*

The Lower Dan Tian and Snow Mountain Area are essential for energy, stamina, vitality and long life. The Lower Dan Tian is also the seat of the soul and a source of energy for the soul. The Snow Mountain Area is the source of energy for the kidneys. It also nourishes the brain and the Third Eye. Developing strength in these two energy centers will increase your ability to open your soul communication channels.

To strengthen your Lower Dan Tian and Snow Mountain Area is to strengthen your body. This is very important. When you do soul communication, you are connecting with the Divine, the highest saints and many other souls. Their frequency, vibration and light are very strong. They have a great impact on your physical being. You can become tired, even drained. A strong body will empower you so that you will not be "knocked down" by the experience of soul communication.

Opening the Message Center

The Message Center is the key energy center for soul communication, so opening your Message Center is essential. The mantra San San Jiu Liu Ba Yao Wu (Chinese for the sacred healing number 3396815[8]) is the mantra for communication. This mantra is a divine code to assist in opening the communication channels for humanity. It is a key for all forms of soul communication. San San Jiu Liu Ba Yao Wu connects with messages in the Soul World. These messages are directly connected with the ability to do soul communication. Use this mantra often. Use it throughout the day.

Ask San San Jiu Liu Ba Yao Wu to open your soul communication channels more completely. This mantra is a direct connection with the Divine and the entire Soul World. It was received by my most beloved spiritual master and teacher, Dr. Zhi Chen Guo, more than thirty years ago. It has been used by millions of people to open their soul communication channels, to offer healing and to uplift their soul standing. This mantra is an absolute treasure for opening your soul communication channels.

Let's practice. Put your left hand over your chest, with the palm facing your Message Center. Put your right hand in the prayer position, with the fingers pointing upward. Place the tip of your tongue near the roof of your mouth. Sit or stand as you did for the Lower Dan Tian and Snow Mountain Area practices. Standing accelerates the opening of your soul communication channels. This is Body Power.

Next, say *hello: Dear soul, mind and body of my Message Center, I love you. You are the key center for soul communication, healing, love, forgiveness, transformation and enlightenment. You have the power to open fully. Do a good job. Thank you.* This is Soul Power.

Visualize a golden, rainbow or purple light ball rotating in your Message Center. Visualize the light radiating in a powerful way. Keep this visualization in your Message Center. This is Mind Power.

At the same time, chant *San San Jiu Liu Ba Yao Wu,* pronounced "sahn sahn joe lew bah yow woo." This is Sound Power. Repeat this mantra as fast as you can. If the sound becomes blurred, that is good. Do not worry about it. Allow it to happen. If the sounds do not become blurred, that is also good. Do not worry about it. Continue chanting. You can also chant *light.* You can chant *love, open, thank you.* You can use other mantras, but San San Jiu Liu Ba Yao Wu is one of the most powerful and most important mantras for the Soul Light Era. Do this practice at least three times a day, for at least three minutes each time. If you can practice longer, do so at every opportunity. The longer you practice, the better. Close with gratitude: *Thank you. Thank you. Thank you.*

To develop your energy centers and to open your soul communication channels, you can also use the healing blessings from my soul in *Soul Mind Body Medicine*.[9] This will greatly accelerate your progress. It is my honor and privilege to serve you in this way.

Soul Language

The Soul Language channel is the foundation for the other soul communication channels. To open your soul communication channels, it is essential to first develop Soul Language and the ability to translate it. There is an entire section on Soul Language in my book *Soul Wisdom I*.[10] Here I will only explain the essence of developing Soul Language.

When you develop any energy center or any spiritual capability, use the Four Power Techniques. For Body Power, put your left hand over your chest, with the palm facing your Message Center. Put your right hand in the prayer position, with the fingers pointing upward.

For Soul Power, say *hello: Dear soul, mind and body of my Soul Language, please come out. Dear soul, mind and body of my Message Center, please receive and express my Soul Language. You can do it. Do a good job. Thank you.*

For Sound Power, chant *San San Jiu Liu Ba Yao Wu.* It is very important to chant this faster and faster and faster. As you increase the speed, stop thinking about the words. Forget about pronouncing the individual words clearly. Focus only on chanting faster — as fast as you can. When you do this, the words will become blurred. They will be replaced by a strange sound. Congratulations! This is Soul Language. Continue chanting your Soul Language. It will not sound like anything you have heard before. It will not sound like another person's Soul Language. It is unique to you. It is unique to your soul.

As you are chanting *San San Jiu Liu Ba Yao Wu,* visualize the brightest light in your Message Center. This is Mind Power.

Continue this practice for at least three minutes. The longer you can do it, the better. For beginners especially, practicing at least fifteen minutes per time would be very helpful. The most important secret is to keep your focus on the heart and soul of Soul Language. The instant your focus shifts to your mind and to how the sounds are coming out, you will lose your connection with Soul Language. This is a mistake made by many beginners. They focus on the sound of their Soul Language, or on the strangeness of those sounds. This focus will stop the flow of your Soul Language, so shift away from this focus as soon as you recognize it. Return to focusing on the heart and soul of Soul Language.

I emphasize again the importance of keeping your focus on the heart and soul of Soul Language and on your Message Center. Go "into the condition" of Soul Language. *Become* Soul Language. When you follow these very simple directions, you will be able to develop Soul Language. The quality of your Soul Language will improve.

Soul Language can be used in many ways. I describe them in my book *Soul Wisdom I.* I recommend that you read that description. Soul Language is absolutely the foundation for opening your spiritual channels, which are the soul communication channels. Soul Language is the most powerful tool for developing your soul communication channels.

When you open your soul communication channels, you have connections with the Divine and the entire Soul World. This is a privilege that is beyond words. To realize we have the possibility of connecting soul to soul with Ling Hui Sheng Shi (Guan Yin's new name in the Soul Light Era), Jesus, Mary, Taoist saints and teachers from other traditions is to appreciate how special the gift of soul communication is.

A single open soul communication channel is healing, rejuvenating and deeply transforming. It gives you access to teachings, wisdom and practices from the Soul World. You become a voice for their messages. This is a most extraordinary privilege. You become a voice to explain their images. This is also an extraordinary honor. Your own soul journey accelerates. All that you receive from the Soul World transforms your soul standing. Your frequency becomes more attuned to the highest frequencies in the Soul World.

You must be committed to developing this ability. You must practice for the same reason a concert violinist must practice. The ability may be there, but without practice it cannot improve. It is very sad to think that these connections can be made and yet some people would not cultivate them through practice. Their souls would be very unhappy. High-quality soul communication is the soul's desire.

Pay attention to your soul's desire. The soul is the boss. It will keep sending you reminders until you pay attention. The reminders might be very strong. You could become sick or have an accident. It is not necessary to receive such strong reminders. Follow the teachings in this book and you will be able to avoid these strong reminders. Soul communication is a treasure, a powerful gift and an extraordinary tool — for your own journey and for serving others, Mother Earth and beyond. We are very blessed to have this opportunity. Use it well.

It is an amazing honor and privilege to receive soul communication. You are participating in a profound conversation. Often your soul will understand much more than your mind. Your soul and your mind will receive great teachings, healings and blessings. Keep a record of your soul communications. Review what you have received every few months. Be sure to always record in some way your most significant or unusual soul communications.

When you first receive soul communication, your response will be surprise, amazement, gratitude and appreciation. You will understand on one level the content of the communication. However, even the simplest and most direct soul communications contain much more than you can appreciate at first. When you review your soul communication a few months later, you will understand it at another level. With practice, the level and depth of wisdom you receive and the frequency of your connection with the Soul World will grow. The benefits of a soul communication practice are almost without limit. Soul communication will accelerate your soul journey significantly.

Developing Your Communication Channels

The suggested practices in this chapter and the next chapter are powerful ways to develop your soul communication channels. It doesn't matter whether your primary channel is through words or through images. Your soul always wants to improve its soul communication channels. There are no limits to this possibility. If you can communicate with the Divine, that means there are no limits. You can never say, "I have fully opened my channels. I receive full and complete messages from the Divine. I see all the images in the Soul World." These statements can never be true. There is always the possibility of receiving more. This is one of the beautiful and exciting aspects of soul communication. No matter how highly developed your ability is, you can always improve. There is always another layer of wisdom, teaching and practice.

There are no limits to the Divine. This means there are no limits to soul communication. The highest saints have a standing so far beyond ours that we can continue to learn from them for lifetimes. The universe has countless secrets. You can connect with these secrets for lifetimes. Moreover, there are countless universes; the stars and the planets cannot be counted. For those who have a special connection with animals, there are countless creatures on Earth and in the sea. These examples help you understand that the possibilities for opening your soul communication are without limit. You can choose any of these sources for communication. You can choose a variety of sources. Any soul that exists can be a source for communication.

At this point, I want to emphasize the need to continually develop your soul communication channels. Keep the countless possibilities in your awareness. This awareness helps you open your channels more fully. It also helps you maintain flexibility. Flexibility is extremely important. You may have noticed by now that I continually refer to all souls. Many people are accustomed to being a channel for only one soul. This is a major difference between my teachings and other teachings. I honor all other teachings. We are all one family. We are all working to bring greater light and love to Mother Earth and beyond. We simply approach this issue in different ways.

My approach is to be open to the entire Soul World. You may ask if this includes the Dark Side. The answer is yes, be open to the Dark Side. However, I must give you a very clear instruction: **Do not use soul communication to connect with the Dark Side.** You can cause great damage to yourself and those you love if you connect with the Dark Side. You are not strong enough to do this. I repeat: Do not communicate with the Dark Side. Do **not** initiate this communication. Sometimes people who are very sincere and kindhearted overlook this caution. They do not pay attention. They make the connection with the Dark Side. The result has been great suffering for them and those they love. Communicating with the Dark Side can damage your health. It can even take your life away. This is how powerful soul communication is. This is how powerful soul-to-soul connections are.

Do not forget this caution. Always use this caution as a guideline for your soul communication. Always remember that when I talk about being open to the Soul World, I always mean the Light Side. I will not continue to repeat this caution or remind you about it. You need to remember for yourself. **You need to always add *"except the Dark Side"* when you read the words "communicate with all souls."**

Benefits of Soul Communication

Soul communication can serve you for healing, prevention of sickness and rejuvenation. With soul communication you can receive teaching from the Divine and from the spiritual world. I will offer more teaching and practice to empower you to receive these benefits in the rest of this book. What I want to emphasize now is that soul communication can be applied to benefit any aspect of your life. Soul communication can be applied any time, anywhere. You can apply and receive the benefits of soul communication wisdom just as naturally and routinely as you sit down to three meals a day and go to sleep at night.

Let me give you a few examples of how to use soul communication in daily life. Just after waking up, and before getting out of bed, you can do the following soul communication: *Dear Divine, dear my spiritual guides and teachers in the physical world and the spiritual world, I love you. Could you give me guidance and a blessing for my work and service today? Please bless me with your love and light. Give me the energy and intelligence to allow me to do a better job of serving humanity. Thank you. Thank you. Thank you.*

If your spiritual channels are open, you can instantly hear the guidance from the Divine and your spiritual teachers in Heaven. If your spiritual channels are not open, if you cannot hear and you cannot see through your Third Eye, you still receive great benefits from doing this soul communication. You have sent your request to Heaven. You have expressed your intention. Your spiritual guides and teachers are delighted to bless your daily life. Your spiritual fathers and mothers will happily assist your requests. You can ask about issues related to any aspect of life, including your health, guidance to support your family, how to improve your work and also how you can serve humanity. The more sincere you are with your requests, the more likely your soul guides will assist you. You will discover that the more service you offer to humanity, the more your requests will be fulfilled. Your life will be blessed.

After breakfast, you may drop your children off at school. Before you leave home, do the following soul communication: *Dear soul, mind and body of my car, I love you. Please run normally and give us a safe trip. Dear God and all my spiritual fathers and mothers in Heaven, please bless our safety.* Imagine what these two sentences could do for your life. It could help you avoid a serious auto accident. Wouldn't that benefit be priceless?

During the ride to school or at any time, do a soul communication with your children as follows: *Dear Kirk and Alicia, I love you. Dear Divine and all my ancestors, I love you. I'm very honored to ask the Divine and all of my ancestors to bless my children. I want them to deal with their classmates with great love and compassion. I want them to understand their great opportunities to learn knowledge to prepare to be a good servant for humanity in the future. I am very grateful for this blessing from the Divine and from my ancestors. Thank you. Thank you. Thank you.*

The moment you do this soul communication, your ancestors will rush to help your children. You may never really know or understand how your ancestors can bless your children, but just think about how much you love your children and grandchildren. Your ancestors have the same great love for you and your children. Your children and you will receive great benefits from this soul communication.

As soon as you arrive at your workplace, do soul communication before beginning any work. It takes only one minute, but this minute will make your life much easier. Communicate as follows: *Dear soul, mind and body of my boss and my colleagues, I love you. Let us communicate well in the physical world to accomplish our tasks today. Dear Divine, dear my spiritual fathers and mothers, please bless my work today. Dear soul, mind and body of my computers, telephones and other equipment, I love you.*

Please function properly to assist me to complete my tasks. I am very grateful. Thank you.

This soul communication to your boss, colleagues and equipment will help create harmonious teamwork and remove blockages from the functioning of your computer and telephones. Your work environment, work relationships and the flow of your work day will be much smoother.

In summary, soul communication can benefit every aspect of life. Remember that pure love is a key for soul communication. Give love, care and compassion to everyone and everything. Ask the Divine, Heaven, your spiritual fathers and mothers, your ancestors and loved ones, your colleagues and boss to bless you and your life. The potential benefits are unlimited.

Soul communication can serve you any time, anywhere for anything. This is why it is so important to learn the wisdom of soul communication and to open your spiritual communication channels, including the Soul Language channel, Third Eye channel, Direct Soul Communication channel and Direct Knowing channel. I offer my personal spiritual calling to each of you. Do the practices that I reveal and share in this book often. Open your spiritual channels. Communicate with the Divine and the universe. Benefit every aspect of your life.

Soul communication is particularly important in this time of Mother Earth's transition. Soul communication is vital for healing. It is also very important for rejuvenation. It could transform your entire life quickly. It could enlighten your soul quickly. I wish that soul communication will serve your life well. I wish that soul communication will transform your life.

❀ ❀ ❀ ❀

As you communicate with all souls, you receive amazing benefits. Your frequency, vibration, quality of light and soul standing increase more than you can imagine. It is beyond your ability to fully comprehend. Follow the suggestions I make. Do soul communication. Practice often. Keep a journal. Your experiences will be your teacher. Your experiences will help you understand how extraordinary and how transforming soul communication is.

I cannot emphasize enough the importance of practicing. Choose a particular time every day as your time for soul communication. Keep this time sacred. A daily practice of soul communication is just as important as a daily practice of eating or sleeping. We do not usually think of eating and sleeping as practices, but in fact they are. They are practices to keep our bodies healthy. Sometimes we need to change our diet to help restore health. Sometimes we need to sleep more when we are fatigued. Eating and sleeping are essential practices to restore, maintain and develop physical health.

Soul communication is also a practice. This practice is one of the ways we can reach a very high level of spiritual health. We can restore, maintain and develop our soul standing. Soul communication is a powerful way to do this. Stop and think about it. For a half-hour every day, or even just ten minutes, twenty minutes or whatever you choose, you can sit in divine presence. You receive direct teachings. You are being tutored by the Divine, or one of the saints, or the soul of a universe.

Receiving this direct teaching transforms your frequency and purifies your soul journey in a profound way. It touches the deepest parts of your life. It reveals things that have been hidden. It manifests gifts that have not been recognized. It brings to your awareness aspects of your journey that need healing. It raises your frequency and vibration. When this happens, you are being restructured. You become stronger, healthier, rejuvenated. You have greater vitality, stamina and the possibility of long life. What priceless treasures!

You receive teachings tailor-made for your soul journey. They can be specific teachings on things you need to correct, areas where forgiveness is needed, or ways to express love unconditionally. These are also extraordinary treasures. All of this is offered to us by the Divine, by the saints and by all souls. Practicing and developing soul communication not only benefits you; it also benefits all humanity, Mother Earth and beyond.

Practicing soul communication develops this ability, like rolling a snowball down a hill. When you begin, your communication might be limited or on a lower frequency. The more you practice, the higher your frequency becomes. The communications you receive become more accurate. The transformation in your frequency has many benefits. When you do soul communication, you receive the messages that match your frequency. Let me give you an example. If three people who have opened their soul communication channels are asked the same question, each one's response will be a little different. The essence of their responses will be the same, but the way that each one expresses the response will be different. The higher the person's frequency, the more complete the response will be. If it is a simple "yes or no" question, the accuracy of the response will be affected by the person's frequency.

This does not mean that one person's response is better or worse or less correct than another person's. It only means that it is from a different frequency. It is similar to having three glasses of different sizes. If you fill each one, each one is full. One glass is not fuller than another. Each one is complete. This is true for soul communication. Each response received is complete. Each response is good and appropriate to the person receiving it.

Practice as often as possible. Increase your frequency. Receive more detailed information. Receive more information that will accelerate your soul journey. Receive deeper teachings and wisdom, and more profound healing. It is quite amazing to realize that soul communication has so many extraordinary benefits. It does not cost you one cent, yet the benefits are priceless. They are treasures beyond your comprehension.

I have identified some of the benefits, but human words are limited. You cannot truly comprehend how priceless the benefits are just by reading this book. The best way to begin to gain a true understanding is to practice soul communication daily. Practice throughout the day. Your experience will be your teacher. Your experience will bring about the transformations I have identified. As you become aware of the profound changes in your soul journey and every aspect of your being, you will have begun to appreciate the full power and benefits of soul communication.

The Soul Light Era

We are at the beginning of the Soul Light Era. This era began on August 8, 2003. The Soul Light Era is characterized by the soul being in charge. The previous 15,000-year era was characterized by the mind being in charge. This shift began only a few years ago. Although we are only at the beginning of this new era, many have already felt the significance of the shift. Many have been moving in the direction of appreciating the importance of the soul, realizing that the soul directs all aspects of life. However, some who have been moving in this direction for several years may still experience difficulty in allowing the soul to truly lead.

In this new era, it is essential to develop soul communication abilities. You must open your soul communication channels more and more fully. This will empower you to participate more completely in the Soul Light Era. Part of your participation is to offer service. Soul communication is itself a very high form of service. It is especially important at this beginning stage of the Soul Light Era. At this moment, only a limited number of people have developed soul communication capabilities to a high level. As this era unfolds, many will develop this ability.

As the Soul Light Era continues, the transformation of humanity, Mother Earth and beyond will be profound. Much that is now familiar will change. Organizational structures, major institutions and even governments will change. The way things are done will change. As the Soul Light Era progresses, everyone and everything will come to the realization that the soul is in charge. With this realization will come a change in the way things are done. This applies to personal decisions and individual behavior. It applies to groups and nations. It applies to Mother Earth and beyond. We cannot even imagine what this means at the moment. It is beyond words.

However, we can pay attention to changes in our personal lives. We can be aware of changes in the groups we belong to. We can notice the shift in the way some governments approach decisions and the shift in their behaviors. All of these are clues as to what is coming. All of this helps us appreciate the fact that in this era, it is the soul that leads and makes the decisions. Perhaps the easiest place to see and experience this is in our physical health, through the power of soul healing. Another area of change is our attitudes, mindsets, beliefs and attachments. As we experience personal changes in these areas, they give us teachings about the power of the soul. They help us understand the possibilities. They help us realize there are no limits on the possibilities that are connected with the soul.

In the Soul Light Era, a number of very high saints are in charge. This does not mean that other saints are no longer important. Some who were in charge in the previous era are also in charge during this one. Some are now "retired." They still contribute. They are still important. However, they are not on duty. For them, this era is, relatively speaking, a time of rest. Is it not sweet and kind of the Divine to put a different group of highest saints on duty at this time? These highest saints use soul communication in a powerful way. They direct and assist us through our soul communication channels. They help us develop our channels. They are present with all humanity in a unique and powerful way. I will describe their presence in a future book in my Soul Wisdom series. At this time, I simply tell you that their presence is unique and powerful. They are helping humanity move forward into the fullness of the Soul Light Era. This fullness will take some time to become present on Mother Earth and beyond.

At this moment, Mother Earth and humanity are at the beginning stages of a new dawn. However, everything will accelerate extraordinarily quickly in the Soul Light Era. Transformation is already occurring on Earth in soul time. It will not take decades, much less centuries, for the fullness of the Soul Light Era to shine upon Mother Earth and beyond. We will pass through the new dawn relatively quickly, although that does not mean in weeks or months. Rather, think in terms of the past. Historically, how many centuries has it taken for an era to develop and come to its fullness? The Soul Light Era will be different. The transformation of the new dawn to the full light of day will not take centuries.

You who are reading this book will probably experience the fullness of the day. This does not mean the full potential or completeness of the Soul Light Era. It simply means we will have passed through the dawn into the light of day. During the dawn, you may experience disorientation, confusion, conflict and chaos. In this time of transition of humanity and Mother Earth to the fullness of light, there will be major challenges for everyone. These challenges will be external and internal. This is the process.

We are honored and privileged to live at this time. We have the opportunity to help accelerate the coming of the fullness of light. We can help ourselves and others achieve clarity and escape disorientation, confusion, conflict and chaos. I could say much more about the Soul Light Era. For now, I simply want to give you an idea of the significance of the current time. I want you to know that we are in transition.

You know that the soul is in charge during this era. Does that mean the mind is not important? Of course not. It does mean that the mind will work in harmony with the soul. The mind will no longer be in charge. It will no longer set the agenda. The mind is still important. It will help formulate and implement the agenda, but it is not the leader to determine the agenda. This shift is very important.

Some of you will find it difficult to make the transition to approaching everything from the perspective of the soul. My suggestion is to use every opportunity to adopt this approach. This will make the transition much easier for you. It will be clear. It will be simple to understand. If you hang on to the concept that the mind is the decision maker, you will encounter barriers and difficulties in your transition to the Soul Light Era. Why make your path more difficult? Relying on logical thinking, when it makes your journey more difficult, is not a good choice.

You might ask, "How can I allow the soul to be in charge?" The answer is simple: *do soul communication.* Do it at every opportunity. Whenever you are struggling with a choice or decision, whenever you have a question, whenever you are confused, upset or discouraged, use soul communication! Whatever is happening in your life, use soul communication! Let this last sentence be a mantra for you. Post it around your home, your work space — wherever you are. *Use soul communication.* It works for everything. There is no question, no situation and no decision that cannot be resolved through soul communication.

There are, however, some questions and situations for which soul communication is not appropriate. I explained them in the book *Soul Study*[11] and will mention them briefly here. It is not appropriate to do soul communication to get information about another person. You may certainly ask questions about your own soul journey. If you are doing soul communication for someone who comes to you to learn about his own journey, that is quite all right. However, if someone comes to you to ask about someone else, that is not all right. We cannot interfere in someone else's soul journey. To do so would break *ling fa*, spiritual law. Breaking *ling fa* is much more serious than breaking human law. The consequences can stay with your soul journey for lifetimes. So, be very careful to follow these teachings. Avoid using soul communication for situations where it is not appropriate. Avoid asking questions that are not appropriate.

Avoid asking about the outcome of a political process. It is also important to avoid influencing the process by doing soul communication for one side or the other. This does not mean that you cannot have a role or interest in politics. You can always send blessings. You can always invite others into God's light. You can always offer unconditional love. You can always offer and receive unconditional forgiveness. However, you cannot use soul communication to influence the result of any political event.

You should not use soul communication in police work. Some who are called psychics do this as their profession. That is their choice. My teachings, which I have received from my most beloved teacher and spiritual father, Dr. Zhi Chen Guo, are very clear. *Do not use soul communication in police investigations.* Those who are subjects of police investigations usually have huge karma. Do not interfere with their karma. It is a serious mistake to interfere with the karma of others.

Some people in the goodness of their hearts have interfered with others' karma. Their suffering has been immense. Their health and the health of family members and even their pets have been affected. I am telling you this as a caution. When you know these things, you can avoid making big mistakes. We all make mistakes. That is part of being human. However, there is no need to repeat the mistakes of others. Learn from them. Pay attention to my cautions. Avoid breaking *ling fa*. The three areas I have identified are the ones where it is not appropriate to use soul communication.[12]

I have given you important information about the Soul Light Era that is directly connected to opening your soul communication channels more fully. All of it helps you develop your soul communication abilities. Knowing that we are in a new era is important. The fact that it is the Soul Light Era makes it clear why it is essential to develop your soul communication abilities. It is clear why you need to open your spiritual channels more and more. Using soul communication, you can receive teachings about this era. You can receive clarity and eliminate confusion. You can help others go through the transition. You will have a more complete understanding of what this era means. These are all special gifts. With these gifts, you will continually grow in your ability to connect with the essence of the Soul Light Era. You will deeply understand that soul communication is the primary means of communication in this era.

As the Soul Light Era continues, logic and the mind will continue to serve. However, answers and solutions will be received through soul communication. Instead of spending hours, days or weeks trying to find solutions by logical analysis, solutions will be received within minutes. This is how things are done in soul time.

Universal Service

By now, you should have a clear idea of why soul communication is important. I have given you some ways to develop this ability. There is another way that is essential. Offering unconditional universal service is the most powerful and effective way to open and develop your soul communication channels.

In April 2003, I was honored to receive the Universal Law of Universal Service. I received this law while teaching a workshop at Land of Medicine Buddha in Soquel, California. Suddenly, the Divine came to me. I stopped speaking and bowed down 108 times.

The Divine told me, "I am here to release a universal law to you." I replied, "I am honored to receive it."

The Divine then said, "This law is the Universal Law of Universal Service. It is one of the highest spiritual laws in the universe. It applies to the spiritual world and to the physical world." The Divine then stated the law:

I am a universal servant.

You are a universal servant.

Everyone and everything is a universal servant.

A universal servant offers universal service, including universal love, forgiveness, peace, healing, blessing, harmony and enlightenment.

If one offers little service, one receives little blessing from the universe and from me.

If one offers more service, one receives more blessing.

If one offers unconditional service, one receives unlimited blessing.

Then the Divine paused for a moment before continuing:

There is another kind of service, which is unpleasant. If you offer unpleasant service, which includes killing, harming and taking advantage of others, you will learn lessons.

If you offer a little unpleasant service, you will learn a little lesson.

If you offer more unpleasant service, you will learn a more serious lesson.

If you offer very unpleasant service, you will learn a huge lesson.

The Law of Universal Service transforms every aspect of your life. The more service you offer, the more every aspect of your life transforms. As you offer greater and greater service, your soul communication ability increases. The more service you offer, the more your ability increases. It accelerates by quantum leaps. This is an example of divine generosity. If we offer one small service, it is multiplied and returned to us as virtue, as transformation and as soul communication ability. It is returned multiplied tenfold, a hundred-fold, and even beyond that. We can never outdo the Divine.

I cannot emphasize enough how important it is to offer service. Service is the purpose of life. However, there is a vital additional teaching. True service, the best service, is offered unconditionally. If you do something to receive blessings in return, this is not unconditional service. Your benefits will be very limited. When you offer service because that is your response to life, you are blessed tenfold or more. Offering unconditional service is absolutely essential.

It is important to realize what service means. The qualities that are listed above in the Law of Universal Service are the qualities of an unconditional universal servant. Service is contributing to improve the situation for others. The role of service in opening and developing your soul communication channels cannot be emphasized enough. Your very use of soul communication is service. Doing soul communication will improve your ability to do soul communication. Offering unconditional love is service. It will also improve your soul communication channels. Anything you do to serve will boost your soul communication abilities.

Service can be offered in many ways. It is not limited to activities. In the West, service is associated with *doing*, with belonging to service groups, with volunteering. This is all correct. However, service also includes chanting, giving blessings and living in an unconditional way. All of this is service, because all of this contributes to benefiting others. You do not have to go out and join another volunteer organization. Doing what you currently do in an unconditional way transforms your activities and brings you to a very high level of service.

Why is there a close connection between offering service and developing your soul communication channels? When you offer service, your soul standing increases. Your frequency increases. In turn, your ability to receive messages from the Soul World increases. In some ways, service and developing your spiritual abilities are two sides of the same coin. When you offer service, your abilities improve. When you use your abilities, you have a greater desire to offer service.

Your soul communication is a treasure that you can use to assist yourself and others. Teachings you receive for yourself can be shared with others when appropriate. You will notice that very often the teachings you receive become part of your daily conversation. The wisdom that you learn becomes part of your thinking. Your ideas and your speech will all begin to flow from what you receive from the Soul World. You will be amazed and delighted at how spontaneous this is.

When you begin the process of using soul communication, you do it in a totally conscious way. You formulate a question and receive a response. You are completely aware that you are receiving a particular answer to a particular question. As you use soul communication more, it will be more integrated into your entire life. You will notice that you are considering possibilities that the Soul World suggests to you. You do not always have to make a conscious shift to ask for this information. It can simply become part of the flow of your day.

The more you use soul communication, the faster this process can take place for you. This process is a wonderful gift. It is available to everyone. All you need to do is practice using soul communication at every opportunity. Follow the guidelines that I have given. Always say, "Thank you." Always honor the Soul World for giving you responses. We are blessed and very privileged to be able to receive direct communication from the highest saints. People throughout history have wanted to do this. Thousands, even millions, of people on Mother Earth at this time want this. You do not have to walk one step to gain this ability. It is right in front of you. It is there for you to accept and use. The more you use soul communication, the higher the level of communication you receive. The more you offer service, the higher your frequency is and the higher the level of teaching you receive. This is a blessing for you. It is a blessing for all humanity.

The wisdom that you receive in soul communication is not solely for you. You are holding that wisdom for all humanity. When you have the opportunity, release that information. Release the wisdom and the teaching. The more you release, the more you will receive. The gifts you receive from the Soul World are put in your warehouse of intelligence and wisdom. If you leave those gifts in the warehouse, very soon it will have no more room. However, if we immediately share our gifts with others, we make room for more wisdom, teaching and gifts. Not only does this benefit you, it also benefits all those with whom you share the teachings.

I cannot emphasize enough how important it is to pass along the information you receive. This is great service. However, timing is very important. Not every piece of wisdom and every teaching you receive is meant for every person you meet. You must understand the other person's readiness. Above all, it is important that you answer the other person's question in a focused way. It does not help and it is not good service to simply pour wisdom and teachings over another person. That can be very upsetting. It can actually be harmful. This point about timing is extremely important. Pay attention to what the other person is ready to receive. Your soul and the Soul World will let you know what pieces of wisdom to share. When you receive the message to share the wisdom, do it immediately with confidence and compassion. This is what I mean by sending things out from your warehouse. If you receive a message the other person is ready for the information, do not be shy, timid or nervous about sharing it. Keeping the wisdom in your warehouse makes it impossible for new wisdom to come in.

As you share, confidence and compassion are two qualities to keep in your mind and your heart. It is not enough simply to be confident. You may then give the other person information they have not asked for. If you are only compassionate, you will be too concerned about hurting the other person's feelings and may not give needed information. Confidence and compassion together form an excellent balance that will guide you.

Follow these guidelines and you will be amazed and delighted at the development of your soul communication channels. You will also be surprised at the response of others. Always give thanks to the Divine and to the Soul World when others are helped. Always tell others, "This is a gift to you from the Divine and from the Soul World. It is only my voice." This is extremely important. If you forget this, it will be easy for you to fall into ego. A big ego is the best way to limit soul communication. It is the best way to lower your frequency. Take great care to avoid falling into ego.

As you share, you may at first feel a little uncomfortable with the responses of others. However, remember that soul communication is a service. What you are offering to others is service, and you can simply say to them, "It is my honor and privilege to serve you in this way." These statements will keep in your awareness the true source of your soul communication. It will keep in your awareness the importance and necessity of service. It will keep you moving in the direction of light so that your soul communication can reach higher and higher levels.

As you develop your soul communication channels, your accuracy will improve. The question of accuracy is extremely important. When you start doing soul communication, the accuracy of the messages you receive may be limited. How can you determine whether your messages are accurate? One of the best ways is to ask: *Does this message promote love, forgiveness, peace and harmony? Is this message a blessing? Will it bring healing? Will it add to enlightenment?* These questions are very helpful to determine the accuracy of your messages, but they are not enough. Messages that are not accurate can come in a very sweet and lovely way. They can appear to meet all of the above criteria. You should ask one more question: *Does this message feed my ego?*

Answering this question can be very tricky. You can receive messages of great love and appreciation from the Soul World that are completely accurate. The Soul World does love us. The Divine does love us. They do tell us how loved we are, how cherished we are and how grateful they are for our service. It ends there. If the message continues on to tell you how wonderful you are, how much more special you are than others, or how much greater your abilities are, these are clues that the messages are coming from your mind and, specifically, from your ego. The Soul World does not speak to us in that way. They do tell us of their love and gratitude. However, they do not make comparisons. They do not tell us that we are the best. All of these traps are easy to fall into. These are traps of what I call false messages. They do not come from the Soul World. They are not accurate.

Any time you receive a message like this, know that it is not accurate. Do not be afraid. Do not be worried or nervous. If you receive such a message, simply say, "I am an unconditional universal servant. This message does not match me or my purpose. I will continue to serve. Thank you. Thank you. Thank you." This response will keep you connected to accurate messages. It will keep you connected to being an unconditional universal servant.

I have another very important caution regarding the accuracy of soul communication. The messages you receive must make sense in the practical world. If you receive a message telling you something that will not work in the "real" world, that message is not accurate. It is a false message. Let me give you an example. If you have a good job that allows you to live a comfortable, simple life and follow your soul journey, you are blessed. Your job is a gift to you from the Divine and the Soul World. If you do soul communication and get a message to quit your job, without any suggestion about another job, that message is not accurate. It is what I call a false message. Do not act on a message like this. Even if the message includes a suggestion for another job, explore the new possibility completely before you quit your current job. These simple guidelines will help you to figure out whether or not your messages are accurate. They will be helpful to you and others. They will be aligned with service. They will be aligned with practical daily life.

Your accuracy will improve as you use soul communication. When you first begin, your accuracy will not be very high. That is perfectly normal. Increasing your accuracy is a slow process. Step by step, your accuracy will improve. Be patient, practice, offer service, and your accuracy will improve. Have no expectations. Do not set a goal to have ninety percent accuracy or ninety-five percent accuracy. Doing this is a subtle disguise for ego. Just do the practice and your accuracy will develop the way it is meant to. It will follow nature's way. As your frequency becomes higher, your accuracy becomes higher. As I have said, the best way to increase your frequency is to offer service.

As you are developing your ability, be very careful to avoid comparing yourself to others. This can be very discouraging or very inflating. Either way, it is again a subtle disguise for ego. I repeat: absolutely avoid making comparisons. What you receive is exactly what the Divine and the Soul World want you to receive. It is tailor-made for you. It is a particular gift to you. When you realize this, saying *this is not as good as someone else* is unimaginable. Saying *this is not good enough* is also unimaginable.

Follow these very simple guidelines, teachings and suggestions. You will be amazed and delighted at how quickly your soul communication channels will open and develop.

❀ ❀ ❀ ❀

In this chapter I have taught mostly about direct soul communication. I will give further teachings in the next chapter about images and intuition. Everything that I have taught in this chapter applies to each form of soul communication. The next chapter will explain each of the four forms. You will understand how to apply the teachings in this chapter to each form of soul communication.

To conclude this chapter, I would like to offer you a blessing for your soul journey so that it will be filled with divine light and have a clear path. Say with me: *Dear soul, mind and body of God's light, I love you. Can you please offer me a blessing for my soul journey? I am honored and appreciative. I cannot thank you enough. Thank you. Thank you. Thank you.*

Then, chant *God's light, God's light, God's light, God's light* for ten to twenty minutes. Visualize your Message Center filled with golden light, with soul light, radiating and vibrating in your entire Message Center. Your heart opens widely to receive God's love and light. Allow God's light to fill every aspect of your soul, mind and body, skin to bone, head to toe, every organ, system and cell. Your entire body radiates God's light.

Chant daily to pull God's light into your body for great benefits. Blockages will be removed to bless your spiritual journey. End by saying: *Hao! Hao! Hao!*[13] *Thank you. Thank you. Thank you.* The first thank you is to God. The second thank you is to all your spiritual fathers and mothers. The last thank you is to your own soul.

Notes

[1] The Akashic Records, or Akasha, is the library in which all events and responses from all realms are recorded. Each soul has a dedicated book therein. All of your actions, behaviors and thoughts are recorded in your book, along with the virtue, good and bad, that you have acquired. Human beings with very advanced soul communication abilities can see this library in Third Eye images and access its information through various soul communication channels.

[2] New World Library, 2006.

[3] It may not be one hundred percent accurate, but it will be trustworthy. I will give more teachings about accuracy of soul communication later in this chapter.

[4] A *cun* is a personal unit of measurement from traditional Chinese medicine. It is defined to be the width of your thumb at the joint where it bends. For most people, it is approximately one inch.

[5] See pp. 304–307 of my book *Soul Mind Body Medicine* (New World Library, 2006) for a fuller description of the Lower Dan Tian.

[6] As I taught in *Soul Mind Body Medicine* (pp. 29–37), "Say Hello Healing" is the essence of soul healing.

[7] Ibid., pp. 178–180, for an explanation of healing number sounds.

[8] Ibid., pp. 56–59.

[9] Ibid., pp. 335–336.

[10] *Soul Wisdom I: Practical Treasures to Transform Your Life* (Heaven's Library, 2007).

[11] *Soul Study: A Guide to Accessing Your Highest Powers* (Zhi Neng Press, 1996).

[12] For more on this, see *Soul Study*, pp. 116–119.

[13] Chinese for "perfect," "get well," "wonderful."

How to Do Soul Communication

There are several forms of soul communication. Soul communication connects with and receives messages from the Soul World. Because there are no limits in the Soul World, there are no limits to the ways in which we can receive its messages. This is an important realization. People sometimes limit or even block their possibilities of receiving messages because they have fixed mindsets, attitudes and beliefs about what soul communication is, how it takes place and how it is received. These limits need to be released. You need to be open to all the possibilities the Soul World presents to you. You need to appreciate the channel that is yours. If you have more than one channel, you are blessed. If you have only one channel, you are also blessed. Appreciate what you are given.

The form of soul communication you are given is the gift tailor-made for you. People often develop more than one method of receiving soul communication, including Third Eye, Soul Language and direct soul communication. Each method assists and reinforces the others. Some people develop one primary method of receiving soul communication. Whatever your situation, it is perfect for you. It is the gift the Soul World has for you at this moment. You may develop additional methods as you practice. You may not. That is not important. What is important is to appreciate your gift and to use your gift for service.

Third Eye

One of the ways that many people receive soul communication is through the Third Eye. The Third Eye is the energy center that receives images from the Soul World. It is a cherry-sized energy center located in the area of the pineal gland. Make an imaginary line starting at the top of one ear, and going up and across your head to the top of the other ear. Make another line starting at your nose, going up across your forehead and continuing across your head from front to back. At the point where these two lines intersect, go down three *cun* into your head. This is the area of the Third Eye.

How can you open and develop your Third Eye ability? The best and safest way to do this is to strengthen your Snow Mountain Area first. I gave you a teaching and practice for this in Chapter 1. Review that teaching. Practice as suggested for at least twenty minutes every day, the longer the better.

Besides feeding your Third Eye, strengthening your Snow Mountain Area will greatly benefit your health. Third Eye activity uses a great deal of energy. You can avoid becoming drained, tired and even sick by having strong foundational energy centers (Lower Dan Tian and Snow Mountain Area). A strong foundation will allow your Third Eye to develop in a comfortable way. You might not avoid all discomfort, but you certainly can avoid major problems. I strongly recommend doing daily Snow Mountain Area practice for at least a month before you attempt to open (or more fully open) your Third Eye. I know some of you are very eager to speed the process of opening your Third Eye. You may be tempted to skip these suggestions. That would be a big mistake.

Once you have developed strong foundational energy centers, a One Hand Near, One Hand Far practice[14] is very helpful for opening the Third Eye. Put the Near Hand four to seven inches from your head. Put the Far Hand fifteen to twenty inches from the top of your head. Both palms should face your head. Say *hello: Dear soul, mind and body of my Third Eye, I love you. You have the power to open [or open more fully]. Do a good job. Thank you.*

Visualize golden light in the area of your Third Eye. See your Third Eye filled with golden light pouring into it from all directions. Visualize the light becoming brighter and brighter, stronger and stronger, more and more condensed. For Sound Power, you can use many mantras: *San San Jiu Liu Ba Yao Wu; light, light, light, light; fully open Third Eye, fully open Third Eye, fully open Third Eye, fully open Third Eye; love, open, thank you, love, open, thank you, love, open, thank you, love, open, thank you* are some examples.

Practice for at least ten minutes. Repeat this practice as often as you can. The more you practice, the better the results you will have.

Here is another practice for opening the Third Eye. Sit on the floor in the lotus position, the half-lotus position or with naturally crossed legs, or sit on a chair with your back straight and not touching the chair. Put the tip of your tongue near, but not touching, the roof of your mouth. Place the heels of your hands against one another, with the tips of your small fingers touching each other and the tips of your thumbs touching each other. Open your palms and the tips of your other fingers so that your hands resemble a lotus flower. Say *hello: Dear soul, mind and body of my Third Eye, I love you. You have the power to open [or open more fully]. Do a good job. Thank you.*

For Sound Power, use the mantra Weng Ma Ni Ba Ma Hong. This is a special mantra of Guan Yin, the Bodhisattva of Compassion. Guan Yin's new name in the Soul Light Era is Ling Hui Sheng Shi, which means "Soul Intelligence Saint Servant."

Say *hello* again: *Dear Ling Hui Sheng Shi, dear Weng Ma Ni Ba Ma Hong, I love you, honor you and appreciate you. I cannot thank you enough. Please help my Third Eye open fully. Thank you.* With your eyes barely open, look down at your fingertips. Chant *Weng Ma Ni Ba Ma Hong* for at least ten minutes, the longer the better. With this practice, your Third Eye may open in one or two days. Some of you may need to practice for one or two months, or even longer. Have no expectation. Do not complain. Remember that whatever you receive is exactly right for you. It is your gift from the Soul World.

Next, here is another One Hand Near, One Hand Far practice to open your Third Eye. Sit in the way described above for the previous practices. Place your hands above your head with One Hand Near, One Hand Far as in the first practice in this chapter. The Near Hand faces your head, about four to seven inches away. The Far Hand is fifteen to twenty inches from the top of your head. Keep your hands in this Body Power position.

Say *hello: Dear soul, mind and body of my Third Eye, you have the power to develop your ability to see images of the Soul World. Make the images very clear. Do a good job. Thank you.* This is Soul Power.

Visualize light coming to your Third Eye, radiating and opening your Third Eye fully. Chant *San San Jiu Liu Ba Yao Wu* or *light*. Chant as fast as you can. If you can speak Soul Language, do so. Visualize your Third Eye radiating golden light as you continually chant *San San Jiu Liu Ba Yao Wu, San San Jiu Liu Ba Yao Wu, San San Jiu Liu Ba Yao Wu, San San Jiu Liu Ba Yao Wu*. Visualize your Third Eye filled with and radiating pure divine light. Allow God's light to radiate, vibrate and fully develop your Third Eye. Focus your attention in your Third Eye and concentrate divine light in your Third Eye. Continue to chant *San San Jiu Liu Ba Yao Wu* or *light* for three to five minutes. Practice daily and you will receive tremendous benefits to rapidly open your Third Eye.

To close this practice, visualize your lower abdomen. Chant *San San Jiu Liu Ba Yao Wu* or *jiu*, the number nine in Chinese. Keep your focus in your lower abdomen for at least three minutes. Finally, say *thank you, thank you, thank you.*

This practice is very helpful in opening your Third Eye. After your Third Eye has opened, this practice will help you open it fully. It is essential to close by focusing on your lower abdomen (Lower Dan Tian) to keep yourself grounded and centered. Focusing on the lower abdomen will help you avoid headaches and being drained or otherwise out of balance. Make sure you include this grounding step every time you do this and any Third Eye practice.

I have given you three different practices to assist you in opening your Third Eye and developing your Third Eye abilities. Additional practices can be found in Chapter 3 of my book *Soul Mind Body Medicine.* All of these practices will serve you well. As I said at the beginning of this chapter, before you begin any Third Eye practice, build your Snow Mountain Area first. Doing Snow Mountain practice daily before doing Third Eye practice will greatly assist you in developing your Third Eye ability.

The Third Eye is a form of soul communication. When you use your Third Eye, images from the Soul World are visible. These images can give you helpful information for your soul journey and for daily life. Sometimes these images come slowly and are recognizable. Sometimes they come rapidly and look like a blur. If this happens, simply ask the Soul World to select one or two images that would be most useful to you. To use your Third Eye for soul communication, you need to see clearly. You also need to keep in mind that what you are seeing is an image. When you see a Buddha, it is the image of that Buddha. The Buddha is not necessarily there in front of you. If you see Jesus or Mary, it is an image. Jesus or Mary is not necessarily there with you. This is true for anything that you see through your Third Eye. It is very important to realize and remember that you are receiving images. I am stressing this idea because to realize you are receiving an image is to understand that you need to interpret what you see. You need to ask the soul of the image what its message is.

There have been times when an image appeared and a message was given. The person who had the Third Eye experience forgot this was simply an image. She used the information to make life choices. This was a big mistake. She did not check if her interpretation of the message was correct. The message told her how important she is, how gifted she is, how she is meant to do great and wonderful things. All of these messages are of the type that I have already cautioned you about. When you receive these kinds of messages and they are connected with an image, it is all too easy to be literal. This is one reason you must always remind yourself that this is an image, and that you must ask the soul of this image what the message is and what the teaching is.

When you receive the image, ask yourself this question: *How does this image offer service to this person? How is it related to their soul journey?* If the response comes back with total love and compassion, and offers service, you know this is an accurate message from the Soul World. If the message you receive does not offer service, it is a false message. Use these two questions to guide your spiritual readings using the Third Eye. They will greatly improve your accuracy and develop your ability further.

In this example, if the person had asked the question, she would have heard, "This is testing. This is to find out how carefully you follow the teachings about the Third Eye." Unfortunately, the person did not ask the question and experienced a great deal of suffering. Not all suffering can be removed. It is part of life. However, you can avoid some needless suffering by following my simple suggestions.

When you receive images of and from the Soul World, you have a very special treasure. Honor and appreciate each image. Third Eye images can help you resolve uncertainties and remove blockages in your soul journey. They can help you know the direction you should take. They can help you attain higher levels of enlightenment. They can help you answer questions about your service, your role and your responsibilities.

Sit and meditate with the image. Ask for the message and the teaching. You will receive profound information. If you ask a question of the Soul World and you receive an image, this is a wonderful blessing. You have excellent information that you can interpret and use to guide you in your soul journey or in day-to-day life.

Let me give you some examples. In your workplace, you may have co-workers whom you find difficult. You can ask for images of the past lives that you have shared. When you see these images, you may immediately understand your current situation. The difficulties in your relationship will make sense. The images you receive give you good information but that is not enough. You need to do something with the information. You could call the soul of your co-worker to be present with you. Tell your co-worker's soul that it is your sincere desire to forgive, be forgiven and improve. Tell the soul how much you love him or her. This is very important. Love melts all blockages. If you want the relationship to improve, you must bring greater unconditional love to it. Even if you think you do not want to say that you love the person, you must still make that effort. Do this on a soul-to-soul level. Let your soul speak to the soul of the other person. Our souls desire nothing more than to offer universal service. The very first characteristic of universal service is unconditional universal love. Your soul will be delighted and grateful to offer this unconditional universal love. The soul of your co-worker will respond in kind, with unconditional universal love.

The opportunity to offer service is always a treasure. It is a particular treasure when that service will help bring about a transformation in people's lives, a transformation that flows from love. It is an honor and a privilege to be able to offer this kind of service.

I could give you many examples connected to different kinds of relationships. You may have some difficult family relationships. Use the same practices to bring love to those relationships. Remember that forgiveness is the mirror image of love. When you offer love, you must also offer unconditional universal forgiveness. Your soul will offer forgiveness to the soul of the other person. You may also need to ask for forgiveness from the other person. This is extremely important to bring about transformation in relationships. Without forgiveness, the relationship will not transform.

Unconditional universal forgiveness brings its own gift, which is deep inner peace. Offering forgiveness and requesting forgiveness opens all the doors to deep inner peace. It releases many mindsets, attitudes and beliefs that have been a heavy burden. With this release, there is an extraordinary sense of freedom. This is authentic freedom that comes from the expansion of forgiveness and love. Nothing else can bring this authentic freedom to you in the same way.

People try hard in many ways to have freedom in their lives. They often say, "I would love to be free of worry, of doubt, of anger…" That freedom and more is waiting for each person. Authentic freedom can be achieved in a very simple way. Simple does not mean easy, but it does mean it is doable. You only have to follow these teachings. The transformation that will come to your life is well worth the effort. Deep inner peace is a priceless treasure.

Many people spend days, weeks and months in an effort to achieve this quality of peace. The secret is to offer and to accept unconditional universal forgiveness. When you receive Third Eye images letting you know that forgiveness is needed, act upon that information. When the Soul World gives you a treasure, accept it. If you do not accept the Soul World's treasure, the Soul World will be reluctant to give you another treasure, because you have not shown appreciation or gratitude. You have turned away. Why would the

Soul World continue to give treasures to a person who continues to turn away?

One way to make sure you are ready for these treasures is to ask only questions that you are ready to act on. If you are not ready to do something with the answer, do not ask the question. Once you have the information, you must use it. Sometimes the information will be presented to you even without your asking. You may receive images that surprise you. Your first reaction might be, "I am not ready." Let me tell you very clearly: if you receive the information, even if you did not ask, you are ready. The Soul World will never give you more than you can handle. The Soul World is infinitely kind and compassionate. You will never be overburdened. If you have received an image, you will also receive the blessing to act upon it. You can absolutely count on that.

These are a few examples of how you can use Third Eye images in your daily life. You can also use them for very practical aspects of daily life, such as finding items that are lost. Not everyone has this Third Eye ability, but with practice you can develop it quite nicely. This can be very handy. Frequently things like your car keys or work papers get lost. When you ask for a quick Third Eye image, you will often be able to see exactly where you left them or where another person moved them. This use of your Third Eye ability can make life less stressful. A word of caution, though: avoid overusing your Third Eye ability in this way. When you realize that you misplace things often, part of the teaching for you is to change your behavior so that you will find the things you need. All of the events in our lives are opportunities to learn and to improve. Everyone loses things from time to time. It is part of life. However, if it becomes chronic, there is a lesson there. Pay attention to the lesson and act upon it.

Another very important use of Third Eye ability is as a medical intuitive. As your Third Eye ability develops, you will be able to see problem areas within yourself and others. This is very helpful, as it guides you how to heal yourself and others. You will also be able to observe the changes that take place with healing. Other images may accompany your Third Eye image of the area of blockage. Often, these are images related to the person's soul journey. For example, you may see an image of a past life action that is the root cause of the present illness or blockage. Such an image illustrates, "Heal the soul first; then healing of the mind and body will follow."

If you are doing Third Eye imaging for yourself, you can use any additional information you receive about yourself without any concern. It is a gift to you from the Soul World. If you are doing healings for another person who has not asked for this information, then simply stay with the physical issue. Do not give information that has not been requested. You may receive a great deal of detailed information that you are simply not meant to tell the person. You must use compassion. You must use a balanced approach to healing. When someone comes to you for a physical issue, deal only with that. You are not being dishonest. You are being respectful.

When people are given information they have not requested, it can actually be hurtful to them. The extra information becomes a burden. It becomes a barrier in their soul journey. You should avoid this completely. Simply tell the person about the physical issue and leave it at that. Teach the person what he can do for self-healing using basic techniques of Soul Mind Body Medicine. When the person is ready to hear about the need to offer universal service, then you can explain that love and forgiveness are the golden keys. The person could take weeks and several consultations to be ready. The person could be ready right away. All you need to do is offer the information when the time is right. As you know, when love and forgiveness are offered, peace is the result. Healing happens at an accelerated rate.

When you use your Third Eye images in the ways I have described, great transformation is possible for you. You can experience amazing changes on all levels of your being. Your spiritual standing will increase. Your mindsets, attitudes and beliefs will begin to be released. Your emotions will be more balanced. Your physical health will improve. You will rejuvenate on all levels of your being. Third Eye images can help you in all of these ways.

There are other ways that you can use Third Eye images. For example, you may have a question about your job. You may be trying to decide among three schools that have accepted you. You may be wondering what you will be doing six months or two years from now. In all of these examples, you can request Third Eye images to offer you the information. If you are asking about the future, however, you need to have highly developed Third Eye ability. You also need to have a high degree of accuracy.

In every case, you must also keep in mind that the Soul World is constantly changing. Change is a universal law. The answer that you receive now may be quite different from the answer you will receive three months from now. Your soul journey will be different. Your soul standing will be different. The service you offer will be greater. Your virtue will be greater. All of these changes will influence and change the information you receive. For this reason, it is necessary to confirm on a regular basis what you have received.

You will discover other ways to use your Third Eye ability. I have mentioned some of the most common and most useful ways. They can bring transformation to every aspect of your life. They are ways of offering service to all humanity, Mother Earth and beyond. It is a great honor and privilege to be able to serve in this way.

Soul Language and Translation

Soul Language is a unique form of communication with the Soul World. It is literally the language that your soul speaks. It is the language that every soul speaks. Because Soul Language is an expression of your soul, it changes. Do not be surprised if there is some variation each time you speak your Soul Language. At the same time, do not be surprised if there are occasions when your Soul Language remains exactly the same. Your Soul Language is unique to your soul journey. No two people have exactly the same journey, so no two people will have exactly the same Soul Language.

When you use Soul Language, you are communicating in an extremely pure way with the Soul World. You can express yourself in Soul Language. You can receive messages in Soul Language. Soul Language is the communication vehicle of the Soul World. It is the way the highest saints communicate with each other. It is the way they communicate with us. Using Soul Language is an extraordinary privilege and blessing.

When you use Soul Language, there is no interference from your logical mind, from your emotions, or from your mindsets, attitudes and beliefs. Using Soul Language is an excellent way to avoid getting stuck. It allows you to communicate without concern that your logical thinking is getting involved. I cannot emphasize enough that this is a very pure form of communication. When you use Soul Language, your soul is expressing its desires, its questions and its service at that particular moment. In fact, your Soul Language can express a great deal more. There is literally no limit to the uses of Soul Language.

You may be asking, "What is Soul Language, exactly?" The language of your soul is very different from the language of your logical thinking. It sounds totally different. For many people, Soul Language first sounds like babbling. It certainly does not sound like anything familiar. Most people would have a hard time saying it even sounds like a language. Your Soul Language might be a repetition of the same sound over and over again, especially if you are beginning. Your Soul Language might have great variation. It might sound like a song that is being expressed in sounds that you do not recognize. Everyone's Soul Language is unique.

To open your Soul Language, first say *hello: Dear soul, mind and body of my Soul Language, I love you. You have the power to express yourself. Do a good job. Thank you.* Then, chant *San San Jiu Liu Ba Yao Wu.* This is the mantra of soul communication. Specifically, it is the mantra to open your Soul Language.

Repeat this mantra over and over. Say it faster and faster. As you do this, release your desire to pronounce each word clearly. This is the secret. You must be willing to let the sounds slur. Do not continue to focus on the individual words of San San Jiu Liu Ba Yao Wu. If you do, then no matter how fast you are saying the words, your focus is on the words. This means your logical thinking is completely involved. If your logical thinking is involved, you will block your Soul Language. It is very simple. Just say the mantra. Say it faster and faster. Release the proper pronunciation of the words and you will spontaneously open your Soul Language — a funny, strange, unique and wonderful sound and voice.

If you did not open your Soul Language, repeat these steps until it opens. Also, ask your guides, ask San San Jiu Liu Ba Yao Wu, ask the Divine, ask your soul to open your Soul Language. Your soul will be more than happy to assist you. It has been waiting this entire lifetime, and possibly many lifetimes, to express itself. It is willing, happy and eager to serve you in this way. Just say *hello.* Ask for its help.

Once you have opened your Soul Language, you can use it in many different ways. You can use Soul Language to offer service. As you are chanting, you can allow the chant to turn into Soul

Language. It will increase the benefits of the chanting. It will increase the blessings and the light. You may chant Soul Language for the pure enjoyment of its connection with the Soul World. Every time you use Soul Language, remember to say *hello*. Remember to ask your Soul Language to serve others.

One of the many blessings and benefits connected with using Soul Language is an increase in your frequency and vibration. When you use Soul Language, you are connecting in a very pure way with the Divine and the Soul World. This pure connection increases your frequency. It accelerates your soul journey. It brings transformation to every aspect of your life. You will experience changes on the physical, emotional, mental and spiritual levels. You may notice improvements in your health simply because you are changing your frequency by chanting Soul Language. These are some of the benefits you receive by using Soul Language.

After you have opened and begun to use Soul Language, it is important for you to learn how to translate it. You are receiving wonderful messages from the Divine and from the entire Soul World. What a pity if they were to go untranslated. All of those wonderful treasures would be sent but not received.

To translate Soul Language, say *hello: Dear soul, mind and body of my Soul Language, I love you. You have the power to give me a clear translation. Send the translation to my Message Center. Let it go from there to my brain and my mouth. Please give me the translation now. Thank you. Thank you. Thank you.*

A good method for developing your ability to translate is to record your Soul Language in short segments at most one or two minutes long. Then play the recording. Whatever you receive is a translation of the Soul Language. You may receive a whole sentence. You may receive one word. You may receive a profound experience, perhaps of peace, love or forgiveness. You may receive an image. Whatever you receive, treasure it. Say "thank you." This is the secret to opening your ability to translate.

When you say "thank you," you are open to all possibilities. In order to translate, you must be relaxed. Gratitude is the best way to become relaxed. When you are in a condition of gratitude, everything is open. Your focus remains on receiving the gift of translation. The very instant your focus shifts and you get nervous because you think you have not received anything, you are shutting the door to your ability to translate. That is a big mistake. Avoid it in the way I have just told you. It might seem too simple, but the most profound truths are extraordinarily simple. Of course, that does not mean they are easy. But it does mean you can use the wisdom and that it is very direct, very clear and very simple.

Repeat this process of recording a brief segment of Soul Language and playing it back. Listen to it with your heart and soul. Let your mind relax. Listen to your Soul Language with an attitude of gratitude. If you receive a sentence, that is wonderful. If you receive a word, that is also wonderful. Whatever you receive is wonderful. If the translation comes to you as a profound healing or an image, put that into words and speak the words aloud. There is great wisdom to speaking the words aloud. It will accelerate the process of opening your ability to translate.

If you are sitting there and thinking, "I am not receiving anything. I am completely blank," and you release that thought and remain completely blank, that is emptiness. So, your Soul Language has expressed an experience of emptiness. You have received a message of emptiness. What a wonderful treasure. Put that into words: "The message of my Soul Language is emptiness. This is a special treasure. I am very grateful. Thank you. Thank you. Thank you."

Now you are ready to record another segment of Soul Language and repeat all of these steps. If you continue to receive a message of emptiness, ask what the associated teaching is. Ask what you are meant to learn. If you receive an experience of profound peace, do the same thing. Ask what it means. Ask what the teaching is, how it is part of your soul journey, what you are meant to learn, or what needs to be healed so that you can live in peace all the time. These are the kinds of questions that you can ask when you are receiving very brief translations. These questions will help you expand the translation that you receive.

In general, it can help your translation if your Soul Language is a response to a question. You may ask the Divine, one of your guides or a high saint a general question, such as "What is your guidance for me today?" You may ask a specific question. Then, speak your Soul Language. When you ask your question, be sure you are addressing it to a specific being. *Dear God, dear Universe, dear Ling Hui Sheng Shi, dear Jesus, dear my healing angels…* Then, ask your question. Additional examples of general questions are "What wisdom do you want to teach me?" and "How can I develop my healing ability?" These are just samples. There are no limits. After asking your question, speak Soul Language in response, record it and then practice translating. You will be amazed at what you will receive.

As I have been offering the teachings in this section, I have also been giving blessings to assist you in opening your Soul Language and your ability to translate it. If you still need to open your Soul Language, simply read this section again and again and receive the blessings. These blessings will assist you more than you can imagine.

There are also several very simple practices you can use to further open your spiritual channels. These practices are for the Message Center. This is the energy center which receives messages from the Soul World and which communicates with the Soul World. The more highly developed this energy center is, the easier it will be for you to do Soul Language and translation. Of course, it is not enough to have a highly developed Message Center. You also need to have a high level of frequency for your soul journey. The higher your soul standing, the easier it will be to do Soul Language and translation. All of these work together.

The practices that I will teach will help you. Suggestions I made earlier in this book give you an idea about the importance of service. Using those teachings will bring your soul standing to a higher level. You will receive great virtue when you offer service. However, you must remember that your service needs to be unconditional. Offering service just to gain virtue will not work. This kind of service is very conditional. It is very small. When you offer small service, you get small virtue in return. Your service needs to be unconditional, offered willingly and without limits. When you do this, the virtue you receive is great.

You may ask, "Is it actually possible to offer service unconditionally?" It is! As a matter of fact, it is easier to offer service unconditionally than otherwise. If you are always calculating the benefits of your service, this becomes a burden that weighs down on you quite heavily. You are unable to experience the joy and the light of giving service freely. When you are unconditional in your approach to giving service, there will be a lightness in your mindsets, attitudes and beliefs. There will be a delight in doing your service. When you chant, there will be a heightened sense of gratitude and respect to the Soul World. All this becomes part of your service when you are unconditional.

The more unconditional service you offer, the more you grow. You get a huge return for a very small investment. You will be quite aware of the return. There will be changes in your behavior, attitudes and beliefs. There will be changes in your ego. You will be better able to release attachments. When you notice these things are becoming part of your life on a more regular basis, be very grateful. All of these changes show that your service has been unconditional. They are the benefits of transformation that come from being unconditional. There are many more benefits but these are some of the most commonly experienced.

Offering unconditional service also has benefits that are directly connected with your soul communication channels. One of those benefits is the ability to connect on a higher level with the Divine and the highest saints. Many people have desired for their entire life to have a conversation with God or one of the highest saints. This desire can be fulfilled at this time. One way of doing that is through Soul Language and translation. The Soul World wants to converse with us also. The highest saints and the Divine want to communicate with us. This might be surprising to you, but it is true. They are ready to offer incredible wisdom, knowledge, teaching, practices, healing and more to humanity and to all souls.

Soul communication is a vehicle for the delivery of these gifts from the Divine. When you do Soul Language and translation, and you receive a bit of knowledge or wisdom, you are receiving a gift that the Divine and the highest saints want humanity to have at this time. This is an extraordinary realization. It is a profound privilege to be the ones to receive these teachings, wisdom, healing methods and more. There is no limit to what can be received. The Divine and the highest saints have many things to share with us.

We will never know everything there is to know. That is not possible because the Source is infinite. But we can connect with much more than has been present so far. A wonderful way to connect is through Soul Language and translation. It is a particularly excellent tool because it is so pure. The possibility of distorting the message is limited. What you receive is a treasure. It is for you but it is also for Mother Earth, all humanity and beyond.

When you first begin translating Soul Language, you might think, "I am not getting anything new. This is the same information I have known for many years. This is information that has been taught and understood by others." That may be true. Many of your communications could be in those categories. That is quite all right. The information is still new. I say this because there are teachings, wisdom and healings that the Divine wants very much for humanity to live. These messages are given over and over and over again. They may be the same word. They may the same concept of unconditional love or unconditional forgiveness, but they do have a newness. The intensity of the message is new. The number of times the message is given is new. The importance and necessity of living these messages is new. You must understand this newness in whatever message you receive. You are a bringer of this message to humanity, Mother Earth and beyond.

Never say, "This is the same teaching as before. This is the same that Susan got. This is the same teaching I've read in books many times before." Instead say, "This is so important to the Soul World. There is an urgency about this message. I must do everything I can to live this message and to teach this message. I am honored to be one of the ones the Divine, the Soul World and the universes have chosen to deliver this message to humanity, Mother Earth and beyond. It is an honor and a privilege to receive these messages. There is an urgency to pass the messages along."

For most of you, the most effective way to pass the teachings you receive to others is through your daily lives. Your actions become the teachers. Your attitudes, mindsets and beliefs become the teachers. When you shift all of your being to unconditional love, forgiveness, peace, healing, blessing, harmony and enlightenment, you become an extraordinarily powerful teacher. You become a special presence on Mother Earth for humanity and all souls.

It is an extraordinary gift that all of this can come from Soul Language and its translation. All of this is actually living the message of your Soul Language and translation. It does not do much good to receive a wonderful message and then ignore it. How many of you would ignore a message telling you that your bank account just had $50,000 deposited into it? Even if you did not believe the message, you would look into it. You would not ignore it. When the message is true, you would show it in your life. This is not a perfect comparison, but it helps you appreciate the importance of paying attention to the messages you receive through Soul Language.

Not only is it important to pay attention; you also need to demonstrate the message in your life. This can be done in many ways. A simple and effective way is to make the small changes in daily life that become obvious to you. When you have made enough small changes, those who know you will become aware of the difference. Our interactions with people who know us give us a wonderful way to understand the changes that take place in the soul journey. It is a wonderful way to begin to appreciate on an entirely different level the importance and significance of Soul Language and translation, as well as every other form of soul communication.

Here are two practices to develop your Message Center. You can do the first one either sitting or standing, although my description is for sitting.

Body Power: Put your left hand over your Message Center. Put your right hand in the prayer position with the fingers pointing upward. Sit in a full lotus, half lotus or simply cross your legs. If you are sitting on a chair, keep your back free. Put the tip of your tongue near the roof of your mouth.

Mind Power: Picture your Message Center full of golden light. The light pours in from all directions. If the light changes color, that is fine. It might become rainbow, purple or crystal light.

Soul Power: Say *hello. Dear soul, mind and body of my Message Center, I love you. You have the power to open fully. Do a good job. Receive the messages from the Divine, the highest saints, all universes. Thank you.*

Visualize your Message Center as being full of light, radiating light. Now imagine your Message Center gradually expanding, to the size of your room, then to the size of your home. It continues to expand, to the size of your neighborhood, your town, your state or province, your country, Mother Earth, the solar system, the universe. Chant *San San Jiu Liu Ba Yao Wu* or your Soul Language throughout. After a minute or two, visualize your Message Center gradually returning in size, from the universe, to the solar system, to Mother Earth, to your country, your state or province, your town, your home, and back to your chest.

Close the practice by focusing on your Lower Dan Tian. Keep it there for at least three minutes. This is a very important step so that you will be grounded. If you skip this step, you may feel unbalanced, even unwell, because you will not be fully grounded and centered. Close: *Thank you. Thank you. Thank you.*

Do this practice at least once a day. It takes only three to five minutes. It is not necessary to spend a long time at each stop along the way, although you may enjoy doing that. As you are returning from the universe, visualize your soul and your Message Center receiving blessings at each stop along the way. This practice will help you gather blessings and light from the universe, the stars, the planets, this solar system and other solar systems.

This is a very powerful and profound practice. It will help you open your Message Center more fully. Nothing is guaranteed, however, so have no expectation that you will have a fully open Message Center in a few days. Just continue to do this practice daily and it will assist you.

Here is a second practice for opening the Message Center. It too can be done sitting or standing. I will describe it for a sitting position.

Body Power: Sit in a lotus, half lotus or with simply crossed legs, or sit on a chair with your back away from the chair. Put the tip of your tongue near the roof of your mouth. Put one hand four to seven inches from your Message Center. Put the other hand fifteen to twenty inches from your Message Center. Both palms should face your Message Center. This is an application of the One Hand Near, One Hand Far Body Power technique.

Mind Power: Visualize golden light coming into your Message Center from all directions. You can also visualize white, rainbow, purple or crystal light.

Sound Power: Use the mantra San San Jiu Liu Ba Yao Wu. You can also use the mantra God's Light. You can use your request as a mantra: *Open more fully. Open more fully. Open more fully. Open more fully.* If you are using your request as a mantra, be the commander. Tell your Message Center to open fully. Do this with respect and love as you say *hello.*

Soul Power: *Say hello. Dear soul, mind, body of my Message Center, I love you, honor you and appreciate you. You have the power to open fully. Do a good job. Thank you.*

When you say *hello,* you are expressing both your love and your gratitude. It is quite all right to be the commander because the command flows from your love and gratitude. You need to be the commander or the soul of your Message Center will not pay attention to you. If you are uncertain or unclear, if you do not really believe improvement is possible, your Message Center will know, and so your Message Center will not listen very carefully. In some cases, your Message Center might not want to respond at this particular moment. That is why you need to be the commander. If you are not certain, your Message Center will not be certain either.

Being the commander accelerates the process of developing and opening your Message Center. It accelerates the improvement of your Soul Language translation. These practices are very simple and very helpful. In the first practice, I taught you to close by focusing on your Lower Dan Tian. End the second practice in the same way. Always be sure to bring your energy to the Lower Dan Tian at the end of any practice you do for your Message Center or Third Eye. It does not matter who taught you the practice; bringing the energy to your Lower Dan Tian is essential. It will keep you grounded and centered. It will strengthen your Lower Dan Tian and your being.

These two practices, in addition to recording your Soul Language for subsequent translation, will assist you greatly. Like everything else, these practices also have souls. Their desire is to serve. When you use these practices, they are pleased. They are eager to assist you. They are eager to assist any person who wants to develop the ability to use and translate Soul Language. All you need to do is ask for their assistance and they will give it. You will be kept grounded and centered. You will also be giving a continual supply of energy and light to your Lower Dan Tian, so your physical stamina, energy and vitality will increase.

The more fully you open your Message Center, the more accurate your Soul Language translations are. Accuracy is of course very important. It assists you greatly in your soul journey. Having a more fully open Message Center also connects you to messages of higher frequency, a very pure communication.

Let me give you more examples of the applications of Soul Language. You can use Soul Language for every aspect of your life. Soul Language can help you identify and understand health issues. Through Soul Language, you can ask for the root cause of a particular issue, such as a chronically sore shoulder. When you receive the translation, the response may indicate a need for forgiveness. Continue to ask: "Whom should I forgive? Whom should I ask to forgive me?" It is very important to act upon the information you receive. If your chronically sore shoulder is due to the need for forgiveness, you can do the Universal Meditation for forgiveness.[15]

The need for forgiveness is the root cause for many illnesses. If you are holding onto hurts, the vibration of the cells is slowed. The frequency and vibration associated with that part of your body affect your physical health. Contraction and tightness are connected with hurt. Think of times when people have said things that hurt your feelings. Very often there is an experience of tightness around your heart, or in your stomach, or in your neck or shoulders. If that experience is not released, it can become chronic and a health issue. When you offer or receive forgiveness, the experience of tightness is transformed. The area can relax. The light can flow. The energy can flow. And so, the area begins to return to good health.

What is true for a sore shoulder is also true for serious illnesses. This teaching is precious wisdom. Follow this teaching and there will be transformation on every level of your being. As I have said before, forgiveness brings peace. When you offer or receive forgiveness, you benefit on every level — physical, emotional, mental and spiritual. Your health begins to improve. The emotion that is connected with the hurt you experienced is released. Your mindset, attitudes and beliefs connected with that hurt are released.

When people experience hurt, they often become very guarded and protected out of a desire to avoid repeating the experience. Being guarded and protected makes it impossible to offer unconditional universal love. When you give or receive forgiveness and release everything associated with your experience of hurt, you are allowing every aspect of your life to become more relaxed and more unconditional. This is a great treasure. You are removing obstacles that blocked the light in your soul journey. Your soul standing increases. You have a greater connection to divine light. You become a greater presence of divine light. All of these benefits come from offering and receiving forgiveness.

It is not *your* forgiveness that you offer or receive. It is *divine* forgiveness. Some people have great difficulty offering and receiving forgiveness because they think it must come from them. Realizing that this forgiveness is a gift from the Divine is completely different. You become an unconditional universal servant in a very special way, through the honor and privilege of extending divine forgiveness to others. You are acting for the Divine. You are expressing one of the cherished qualities of the Divine. You are manifesting a characteristic that the Divine wants present on Mother Earth, and which is currently missing in almost every situation. There is such a need to have divine forgiveness offered to others. Being the bringer of this quality is powerfully transforming. It transforms you, and the transformation extends far beyond you to all humanity, Mother Earth and beyond. Every time you offer and receive forgiveness, you are removing obstacles to the presence of divine light. You are participating in the transformation of humanity and Mother Earth. It is truly an honor and a privilege to realize that you have this opportunity.

Many people desire to bring peace to Mother Earth, to heal Mother Earth, to help others who are experiencing difficulties in their lives. All of this is possible when you offer and receive divine forgiveness. This gives you an idea of how powerful it is to offer and receive unconditional universal forgiveness.

All that I have said about offering forgiveness is true when you receive forgiveness. Amazingly enough, some people find it more difficult to receive forgiveness. Their egos have many attachments. These attachments make it difficult for them to say, "I made a mistake and I do need to be forgiven." This is difficult to understand. Forgiveness is an extraordinary treasure offered by the Divine. Why resist receiving this treasure? If someone came to you and offered you a million dollars or even a hundred dollars, I think you would say, "Thank you. I am happy to receive this." In the physical world, money is the measure of value. In the Soul World, forgiveness has much more value than money has on Earth. There is huge virtue attached to receiving forgiveness. You are literally being offered a treasure. The only response that is appropriate is, "Thank you."

However, if your ego has a hard time admitting your mistakes, this is also a treasure. Use Soul Language to ask your ego what it needs to do in order to be grateful for forgiveness. Ask it what it needs to transform. What mindsets or attitudes does it need to release? What attachments does it need to release? The Soul World will be delighted to hear these questions from you. The answers you receive will be very clear, very direct and of high quality. The Soul World wants you to progress on your soul journey. It wants you to live all of the universal qualities. It wants you to accept the amazing divine generosity shown to us through unconditional forgiveness.

If you continue to have difficulty accepting forgiveness, you are slowing down your soul journey. Some people refuse to accept forgiveness because they refuse to admit they are wrong. This is a pity. It is as though they are turning their backs to the Divine. How can you can continue on, much less accelerate, your soul journey if you turn your back to the Divine? This is very serious. The soul journey is a serious journey.

Now, I do not want you to panic if you remember events in your life where it was difficult for you to accept forgiveness. Do not worry. That was in the past. Ask the Soul World and the Divine to forgive you. Say you are sorry, and continue on a new and different path. Take this wisdom and teachings and put them into practice. Dwelling on what you did before is another mistake. It does not help you to move forward. It is actually an attachment. Release the attachment and move forward.

The suggestions I have given are ones that you can apply to other situations. Another suggestion I would make about receiving forgiveness is to speak directly to the soul of the situation. Use Soul Language to ask the situation why it is difficult for you to accept forgiveness. What do you need to release? What do you need to learn? These are very direct questions and you will receive direct responses. If you are just beginning to translate Soul Language, you might receive only one or two words as your translation. That is quite all right. Use whatever information you have and put it into practice.

Let me give you an example of asking for the root cause of a physical issue. If you have a problem with your knees and ask what the root cause is, very often you will be told it is your stomach. This is exactly right. Issues with the knees are often connected with the stomach or the digestive system. This is a direct connection and you have the information you requested.

The next step in healing your knees is to ask what you need to do to heal your stomach. The response may include several actions. You may need to change the way you eat. You may need to change the amount you eat, the kinds of foods that you eat or the time of day that you eat. You may also be told that you need to strengthen your stomach energy, or to release worry. These are just a few of the possibilities.

Let me give you a word of caution about releasing emotions. Sometimes people say, "I am not going to worry. When something that triggers worry comes my way, I am simply not going to worry." Those who have tried this approach know it will not work. Instead, when you are aware that your response is to worry, transform the worry to confidence. Tell the worry that you love it. It has given you good messages in the past, but at this time it is no longer needed. Invite worry to be transformed to light, or to confidence, relaxation or calmness.

The invitation to transform to another emotion is powerful. You are not just telling the worry to go away. You are being respectful. You are acknowledging that it has a soul and you are inviting it to become a presence of something that is more powerful, something that will allow the energy and light to flow, something that will improve your physical well-being, and something that will improve every other aspect of your being.

If you are a beginner at Soul Language and translation, you may not receive full sentences or paragraphs. However, you will definitely receive messages. Ask for more information. With the example of knee pain and the connection with your stomach, you might get the response "food" when you ask how you can help your stomach. Now, there are many different possibilities connected with the word "food," so you can simply begin asking questions. Would it help for me to change what I eat? Then, receive the answer and translate it. If the answer is "yes," then you can ask more questions. If it is "no," go to other questions.

Little by little the amount of information you receive will increase. Use the practices I have described. Do Soul Language and translation daily and you will be delighted with the responses you receive. They are wonderful treasures from the Soul World.

I have given some examples dealing with your physical health. I have given some examples dealing with your soul journey. There are no limits on what you can ask. Just remember that your questions need to be about yourself – your soul journey or other aspects of your life. If someone else has asked you to do Soul Language and translation for them, that is a wonderful service. However, if you have not been asked to do this, you must absolutely avoid asking about other people and their situations.

If you are giving healing blessings and you want to know the best healing blessing to give, you can simply make that request: *Dear soul, mind and body of my Soul Language, please give the most important healing blessing to....* As I have said, your Soul Language is a very pure channel of communication. It is connected with all levels of the Soul World. Your Soul Language will know the appropriate healing blessing to offer.

Your Soul Language and translation will improve the more you practice. You will experience many blessings in your life as you use these wonderful gifts. Develop this ability and the universe is open to you. You are extremely blessed.

Direct Soul Communication (Direct Flow)

Another form of soul communication is what I call direct soul communication or direct flow. In direct soul communication, you receive direct messages from the Divine, the highest saints and the Soul World. The messages you receive are in sentences or phrases that you can understand immediately. In direct soul communication, you will very often hear the words that are being given to you as the message. You may also simply open your mouth and the words will literally flow out. I call this allowing the Divine, the highest saints and the Soul World to "borrow your mouth." You do not think it through. You do not think at all. You simply open your mouth and speak the information that is coming through you. It literally is a message from the Soul World, and the only thing that is yours is your voice, not the words or the message.

How can this happen? Say *hello: Dear soul, mind and body of my Message Center, I love you. Fully open to receive the message. Do a good job. Thank you.* Then, ask whomever in the Soul World you wish to hear from, whatever it is that you want to know. *Dear Shi Jia Mo Ni Fuo,*[16] *I love you. Please send your answer to my Message Center. At the same time send it to my head. Use my mouth, and not my thinking, for speaking. Thank you.* The message needs to be sent to your head so that your speech functions can operate. However, it is not your thinking that provides the answer. Shi Jia Mo Ni Fuo has sent the answer to your Message Center.

Shi Jia Mo Ni Fuo is a universal servant. He will offer you service through direct soul communication. This is one way in which you can communicate with him and all the buddhas, saints and holy beings. You can ask Shi Jia Mo Ni Fuo for guidance or a teaching. Simply ask with sincerity. For example, you can ask: *Dear soul, mind and body of Shi Jia Mo Ni Fuo, I love you. Can you please offer me some guidance for my spiritual journey?* You can ask for guidance each day by saying: *Dear soul, mind and body of Shi Jia Mo Ni Fuo, I love you. Can you offer me some guidance for today?* These are two simple yet practical ways that you can use direct soul communication to communicate and receive messages from Shi Jia Mo Ni Fuo and all of the buddhas, saints, holy beings and healing angels in the Soul World.

You might also want to hear from your grandmother how she is doing. She may be in physical form or she may have transitioned. It doesn't matter because this is soul communication. You can simply say: *Dear grandmother, I love you. How are you doing? What do you want to tell me? Please send your message to my Message Center. At the same time send it to my head. Use my mouth, and not my thinking, for speaking. Thank you.*

Speaking the message is very important. It is especially important for those who are just beginning. You may hear a response immediately. Speak the answer out loud anyway. We are so used to thinking things through silently that it is very easy to slip into that approach and assume that is a direct flow. When you speak the message out loud, you will be amazed that in most cases there will be a difference from your thinking. Sometimes the message you speak out loud will be completely different. Allowing the Soul World to borrow your mouth means that you are willing to speak the message out loud. Many people feel embarrassed when they first begin. Why? It is an honor and a privilege to receive a direct message. It does not make sense to be embarrassed about this. However, I know that some people are. Once again, that is simply an issue of ego.

Up to this point in your life, you may not have been comfortable talking about spiritual ideas. You may think that only special people can receive direct messages. You may think you are not one of those special people. You may not feel comfortable being a special person. You might sense there is a responsibility that goes with this gift. There are many other possibilities. Release all of them. Say "thank you" to them. Invite them to transform to light. Invite them to increase your connection with the Soul World. Invite them to increase your understanding of what a privilege direct flow is.

The kinds of information you receive are without limit. Everything I described in the section on Soul Language and translation is also true for direct flow. You can ask questions about your soul journey, about your physical health or about attachments you need to release. You can receive information about anything that is part of your life through direct flow.

Let me add a word of caution. Direct flow is not a replacement for thinking and decision-making. For example, if you are buying incense, use your logical thinking and decision-making ability to make your choice. You do not need to do a direct flow to guide you. Would you ask God and the highest saints which kind of incense they want you to buy? No. Just make the decision yourself.

If you really want to do a flow on this issue, it would be appropriate to speak to the soul of the incense. Ask the incense which one would serve you best, which one is the best to come to your home at this time. You could get the response that all of them want to come! This puts you right back where you started. You will still have to use your logical thinking and normal decision-making process.

❀ ❀ ❀ ❀

Direct flow is a wonderful treasure. If you are communicating with the Divine, you are actually receiving direct teachings from the Divine. This is amazing. You are being tutored in your soul journey by the Divine. The quality of response you receive is profound. The resulting transformation is profound. The increase in your soul standing is significant.

You have this priceless opportunity every day. I strongly recommend that you set aside a particular time in your day to sit down in stillness and do direct soul communication. There is no greater treasure. There is no more powerful and profound teaching that you can receive. It is an expression of the unbelievable generosity of the Divine to give us this opportunity to receive the teachings needed for our own individual soul journey. Who could imagine such a gift? You can do this every day. You can do this more often throughout the day. However, I recommend that you set aside a particular time when you can do this on a daily basis. Setting a particular time is important because you are expressing your respect, love and gratitude. You are demonstrating that you realize this is sacred, that it is the greatest treasure that you can receive. If you do direct soul communication for a few minutes here and there at random throughout the day, you are not sending the same message. You are not showing the same respect. There will be times when you can also communicate throughout the day in addition to doing your regular set practice. That is quite all right.

As you do a daily practice of direct soul communication, your frequency will become more and more aligned with divine frequency. Eventually, you will begin to live in a condition of direct communication. You will become aware that you are receiving flows throughout the day, even though you may not have asked a direct question. You will eventually live your day in connection with divine presence. Most people who are serious about the soul journey have this as a goal. Living in connection to divine presence is a treasure that is beyond words. It simply cannot be described. Your soul will experience great joy and gratitude. The Divine will also be grateful. Remember that the Divine is an unconditional universal servant. Serving you in this way is a delight for the Divine. When you dedicate time every day to practice, you will accelerate your soul journey more than you can imagine. There are not many other things you can do to bring about such rapid and deep transformation.

You can also communicate daily with the highest saints. You may have special guides, saints, angels or other holy beings who are important in your life. Practice in the same way. Set aside a time during the day to do direct soul communication with them. You might not spend more than fifteen minutes communicating with the Divine and with your guides. Those fifteen minutes are the most important fifteen minutes in your day. Of course, it is also an honor and privilege to be tutored by the highest saints. Very often followers of a particular tradition think, "It would have been wonderful to have lived at the same time as Buddha, Jesus, Mohammed" or whoever. That is true. But you are not limited. You can ask any of them a question and receive a direct response. You can have a daily conversation, a conversation directly connected to your journey. The responses you receive to your questions will be absolute treasures of wisdom, healing, rejuvenation, blessing and transformation.

Some of you may still be wondering how exactly to do this. Let me review the process with you. Sit on the floor or a cushion in a full lotus, half lotus, or with simply crossed legs, or sit on a chair without touching the back of the chair. Put the tip of your tongue near the roof of your mouth. Put your left hand over your Message Center. Put your right hand in the prayer position. Visualize your Message Center as full of golden light, rainbow light or purple light. Visualize the one to whom you will give your question. Then, say *hello: Dear*
____, I love you, honor you and appreciate you. Please give me the guidance I need for this day. My question is ____. I am very grateful. Thank you.
Chant *San San Jiu Liu Ba Yao Wu* three times, and then allow it to become Soul Language. When your awareness shifts, stop the Soul Language and begin to speak in flow the answer to your question. Record it. This is the process. It is very simple.

Remain completely relaxed. Keep your focus on the one in the Soul World whom you have asked for a teaching. Whatever you receive, speak that message. Very often the first word you receive will be "the." This may not seem like a high-level spiritual teaching! However, when you trust what you receive and you say "the" out loud, it is like turning on a faucet. You will start the flow. Your willingness to say the first word will turn on the faucet and other words will follow.

You may get a sentence. You may get two or three sentences. Whatever you receive is a gift from the Divine, from the Soul World, from whomever you ask the question. Be sure to express your gratitude. Avoid comparing yourself to others. Making a comparison is a form of complaining. Complaining is a very good way to stop all progress on your soul journey. It is a very good way to stop the improvement of your flow. Avoid complaining. Replace your inclination to compare or complain with total gratitude.

Whatever you receive in flow is a response tailor-made for you. If you receive one word, that is a treasure. Think of the millions and billions of people who have never received a direct word from the Divine. One word is an honor and privilege. It is to be received with gratitude. Practice gratitude, practice flowing, and your abilities will increase. I cannot emphasize enough how important these responses are. Continuing to practice is actually a manifestation of your gratitude. If you quit practicing, if you give up, your actions express unhappiness. They are a form of complaining. Continue to practice diligently and devotedly. You will be amazed and delighted by the results. Some of you may take more time to develop fluency in doing direct flows. That is quite all right. Continue to be grateful. Continue to practice.

Total GOLD

What I have taught about accuracy of Soul Language and translation is also true for direct flows. It is very important to realize that your direct flows have limited accuracy. When you are beginning, the accuracy might be quite limited. The more you practice, the more service you give, the greater your accuracy becomes. The secret to increasing your accuracy is to be an unconditional universal servant. This includes living a life of total GOLD. Each letter in the word GOLD has specific meaning. G stands for gratitude. O stands for obedience. L stands for loyalty. D stands for devotion. All of these qualities are given from you to the Divine, totally.

With total gratitude there are no reservations. A good way to know whether or not your gratitude is total is the quality of joy connected with it. If you are joyful when you express your gratitude, then in most cases your gratitude is total. When you can delight in the successes of others, your gratitude is total. When you can delight in the abilities of others, your gratitude is total. This quality of joy and light lets you know that you are experiencing total gratitude. If you experience joy that is limited, do not worry; simply keep moving in the direction of becoming completely joyful for everything that is part of your life.

What I have just said about gratitude is true for obedience, loyalty and devotion. Sometimes we are asked to do things by the Divine which are challenging. To accept these challenges with joy and gratitude lets you know that your obedience is becoming more total. There is always room for an increase in the "totalness" of your total response. When we offer these four gifts to the Divine, the possibilities for being total are unlimited. Striving to become more and more total in your response will continue throughout your soul journey.

It is important to understand the meaning of obedience. In the West, people can have a problem with this word because freedom is valued very highly. Many people think that freedom and obedience are opposites. This is not true. Real obedience is the doorway to freedom. This idea is not understood in most of the West. To be obedient is to have a listening heart. You are paying attention to the messages, requests and directions from the Divine with your heart. This is very different than listening from your logical mind. There are times when the Divine will ask things that do not always fit logical thinking or the practical realities of life.

If you receive a request from the Divine that seems as though it does not fit, you must ask your teacher to confirm the message.

It is very important to be absolutely clear on this point. Not every message you receive will be a true message. What you receive as a request, direction or guidance from the Divine must fit with your practical life. When it does not, you must check with your teacher. Very rarely will the Divine ask any person to do something that does not fit with practical life.

Use this caution as a guideline. If you receive a message that does not fit practical life, you need to make sure it is a true message. Sometimes these messages are a form of testing. People who receive directions to do things that do not fit practical life can become very proud. They can fall into the trap of ego. They can begin to think how very special they are. If this becomes your thinking, it is a one hundred percent perfect indicator that you have gone down the path of ego. You have lost your way. You need to redirect your soul journey.

These guidelines are very clear and very simple, so they are actually very easy to follow. Difficulty arises with resistance from your ego. If you receive a message to do something that is not practical and your teacher says, "This is not a true message," release the message. Be grateful for the teaching. Releasing the message can be difficult. This is the challenge.

People on the spiritual journey have a major challenge. That challenge is ego. A message from the Divine or a high saint that tells you that you are special is a perfect and common example of this challenge. If you accept this message as true and act on it, you can create many blockages for yourself. Some misguided people have sold their homes, given away all of their possessions and become homeless. They are then no longer able to serve because they are consumed with survival. This example might seem extreme, even impossible, but it is true. It has happened.

The Divine wants our total obedience but even more, the Divine wants us to be able to give service. The Divine wants us to function in daily life in the physical world. If your message will make it difficult for you to function in daily life, this is a huge signal that the message is not accurate. There is a difference between total obedience and following messages that make participating in daily life impossible. Total obedience does not mean blind obedience. When you make a commitment of total obedience to the Divine, many challenges will come your way. Do not add to them by following inaccurate messages.

Going through the everyday activities of your life and performing them in the condition of total obedience to the Divine will give you many opportunities to respond to life's challenges. Most people put their own priorities first. Offering love and forgiveness is very conditional. Living in total obedience transforms that. Your own comfort and convenience are no longer number one. Your priorities shift to offering unconditional universal love and unconditional universal service. This shift brings great transformation. It is very easy to read these sentences. It is not easy at all to live the message of these sentences.

Total obedience does not mean that you must completely change your lifestyle. It does mean listening at every moment to the Divine and responding with unconditional universal love and unconditional universal forgiveness. The Divine is not asking us to fit forty-eight hours of response into a twenty-four-hour day. This is not total obedience. The Divine realizes the need for balance. This is why yin/yang is a universal law. When you look at the yin/yang symbol, you can see instantly that it is balanced. One flows into the other; one joins hands with the other; and one is contained within the other. This is true for living total obedience in your daily life. One aspect of your life flows into the other. One aspect of your life joins hands with the other. One aspect of your life is contained within the other. To live in a balanced way is to live total obedience. It is being the presence of the Universal Law of Yin/Yang.

Attaining true balance in life is a major challenge. In our modern world, it can be very challenging because the rhythm of life is very intense. The key idea to keep in your awareness is that obedience is having a listening heart. When you truly listen with your heart and not your mind or your ego, you will be balanced. When you listen with your heart, your decisions and choices will match your needs in the physical world. When you listen with your heart, you will respond from the condition of unconditional universal love and unconditional universal service.

To develop this ability to listen to your heart, you can simply ask the soul of your heart to teach you how to do this kind of listening. You can ask it to develop your ability to listen in this way. Listening to your heart will keep you on the soul journey to light. You will avoid struggling with challenges. When you meet a challenge, you will recognize it. You will say, "Thank you. You are a gift of divine love. I am grateful for your presence and your teaching. Please join me on my journey to divine light, on my journey to be divine light."

Using this approach will transform the challenge. It will become a steadfast companion that can assist you in countless situations. These challenges also want to serve. They also want to be unconditional universal servants. They also want to practice total GOLD and listening from the heart. When you respond to challenges in this way, you are giving them a priceless opportunity to transform. Their gratitude and their assistance will be profound and continual. The challenges that are transformed to light will not be able to thank you enough.

As you know from your own life experience, these challenges are strong and persistent. They have great determination. When you invite them to transform and they become your companions, they bring all of these qualities with them. They assist you with their strength, their determination, their persistence and their perseverance. These are wonderful ways to be able to progress in your soul journey. These challenges and all of their special qualities can help accelerate your soul journey in a most amazing way. They can bring depth, intensity and frequency to your commitment to live total obedience. They will assist you through their own efforts to live total obedience.

A listening heart will also help you to be totally loyal. You will know in your heart and soul the wonderful gifts and opportunities you are receiving constantly from the Divine. You will know what an honor and privilege it is to participate in the divine mission. When you know these things in your heart, how can you not be loyal to the Divine?

Total loyalty to the Divine is very important. This quality is often overlooked or not considered in a conscious way. To be loyal simply means that you stand by your commitment to the Divine. Very few people have difficulty being loyal to the Divine. If you are on a spiritual journey, it is an almost automatic response. However, the aspect of loyalty that is often overlooked is to be consistent and persevering in your commitment. This is a very important expression of loyalty. Being loyal means that you can be counted on. This is true in the spiritual journey also. To be loyal means the Divine can count on you. You will be there. It does not matter if the task is pleasant or not, if it is something that gets recognition from the public or not, or if it is something that you would consider a worthy use of your talents or not. None of these considerations is important. What is important is that the Divine can count on you, no matter what the task.

This might seem like a very obvious statement. You may be thinking, "Well, of course, the Divine can always count on me." However, I would suggest that you review your commitment. Review your follow-through on various things you have been asked to do, either by your teacher or by your own guides. Reflect upon those things you have decided are important in your life. When you do this reflection, be kind and gentle with yourself. Do it in a way that is a learning experience. It is meant to be a teaching. It is not meant to be a judgment.

Simply do the review I have suggested. When you find that there are many situations in which you have not followed through, when you have not been consistent with your commitment, realize these are opportunities to learn and to improve. Ask yourself what you can learn from the lack of consistency. Ask your guides and the Divine. Ask the soul of the commitment what makes it difficult for you to be consistent. Use Soul Language and translation to do this. Use direct flow. Use Third Eye ability. Use one, two or all of these forms of soul communication. You will receive precious information and valuable teachings.

When you receive these teachings, act upon them. Do not try to change everything all at once. Choose one area where you know you can succeed. Do not choose the most difficult commitment and say, "I am going to be totally loyal all the time." This is not a realistic approach. Choose something you know you can and will do. Be completely consistent with this commitment. When you have experienced success day after day, week after week, for at least three months, then you can say to yourself the pattern has changed. You can enjoy the fact that you have been completely consistent in this one aspect. You can thank God, your guides, your teachers for assisting you in showing this aspect of loyalty in your daily life.

When you have this success in one commitment, then you can move on to another one. Little by little you can go from the ones that are the easiest to the ones that are most difficult. It is the same process people use when learning to play a musical instrument. They begin with pieces that are easy. They begin with scales and build from there until they are finally able to play very complicated pieces. This is true for your commitments also. Begin with ones that are easy and move forward from there.

Following this process is another opportunity to manifest loyalty. It shows a willingness to follow a process that may not be as glorious as you would like. It may seem a bit boring to start with something so simple. However, this is the way to move to the condition of total loyalty. These are the steps to follow to make your commitment completely consistent. And this commitment is an important doorway to total loyalty. It is not the only way but it is a way that is available to every person each and every day. It is wise to choose something that is doable and available. Follow these suggestions, follow these teachings, and you will experience a great increase in your consistency and commitment. You will move to a response that is total loyalty.

Total devotion is the next essential quality. This quality can be described in many different ways. I would describe total devotion as an attitude of appreciation, respect and reverence for the Divine. This is absolutely important. In the West it is sometimes difficult to enter into this attitude of complete and total devotion. Respect and reverence are not important parts of our society. However, in the spiritual journey, they are absolutely vital. You cannot progress unless you have these qualities and show them at every opportunity to the Divine.

Appreciation is another important quality. It is closely related to gratitude, but there is a little difference, and that is why I have included it as one of the aspects of devotion. These three characteristics of appreciation, respect and reverence will show themselves frequently. You have many opportunities throughout your day to express them.

The total GOLD is for the Divine. It is important to keep this in your awareness. We can never be grateful enough. We can never express our devotion enough. For some of you, it is easy to think of ways of being grateful and obedient, especially if you have had experiences that make you very aware of these responses. This is sometimes not as true for loyalty and devotion. With these teachings on loyalty and devotion, your awareness will increase. It will be possible for you to practice each of these qualities in a much fuller way.

Expressing your appreciation, respect and reverence for the Divine takes different forms. Some people will express them in ways that are very traditional. Others will develop their own means of manifesting devotion in their lives. Many people will combine traditional and their own forms of expression. Some will learn ways to express their devotion from their teachers. Whichever means you use, make sure devotion is part of each and every day. Make sure that you begin your day with total GOLD, that you end your day with total GOLD and that total GOLD is woven throughout your day. Doing this will greatly accelerate your soul journey. It will increase the quality of light in your soul journey. It will increase your frequency and your soul standing.

A very important way to show total devotion is to offer your respect, reverence and appreciation to the Divine before you eat. This is a wonderful practice because most people eat at least three times a day, and many people also have little snacks in between. All of these are excellent opportunities to express your devotion. The more often you express your devotion, the more often you are blessed by the Divine and the easier it becomes to live in the condition of total GOLD.

You will discover your own opportunities throughout the day to express your devotion and the other aspects of total GOLD. All of these opportunities are wonderful treasures for you. They assist you in being the presence of total GOLD. Living this way is the key to the spiritual journey. It is extremely important for developing your ability to do direct flow and all forms of soul communication. When you do direct flow, you can receive your own tailor-made teachings on the significance and benefits of total GOLD for your life. You can receive guidance on how you can develop each quality to a greater degree. As you receive these teachings and guidance, you will also be living total GOLD to a fuller degree. This is very helpful. When you do the flows, it helps you understand and live total GOLD. As you live total GOLD, your flows become more accurate and on a higher frequency. It is a wonderful cycle that continues to spiral out and become more and more filled with divine light.

You can use your ability to do direct flows for many other aspects of your life. This example of using it to learn more about total GOLD gives you an idea about the possibilities. As I have said, the possibilities are almost without limit. The more you practice doing flows, the more possibilities you will discover. Each one is a wonderful opportunity to receive direct teachings from the Divine and the highest saints. They are all special gifts and special blessings. You are very honored. You are very privileged.

Direct Knowing

Another form of soul communication is what I call *direct knowing.* This term is also used in some other spiritual traditions. Like the other forms of soul communication, *knowing* is connected with the Message Center. The more fully open your Message Center and the higher your soul standing, the more able you are to develop this ability. With direct knowing, there is no need to ask a question. There is no need to wait for an answer. You simply immediately *know* the teaching, the information, the wisdom, the guidance. It is there, directly and immediately.

To help you understand this teaching, think about a time when you were in school and your teacher was presenting a lesson. It could be in math, grammar, history or science. The subject does not matter. As the teacher was presenting the material, you had some confusion. You were not really clear on the concepts. You were struggling to grasp the ideas so that you could use the information. As you listened and thought about what the teacher was presenting, you suddenly had an instantaneous understanding of the concepts. You knew what the teacher was saying. This comparison will help you understand the nature of direct knowing.

When you are able to communicate through direct knowing, you instantly understand with great clarity the teaching, wisdom and guidance from the Divine, the highest saints and the entire Soul World. You do not even have to ask a question. You might be going about your daily tasks and suddenly have an insight, an awareness, a *knowing* that you did not have before. This is the type of soul communication that I call direct knowing.

It is quite different from reflecting on something and coming to an understanding. Direct knowing is an instantaneous and crystal clear message from the Divine, the highest saints and the Soul World. The message might involve something that has been part of your daily life. It might involve something that is completely new to you. In almost all cases, direct knowing will come as an insight that is very clear and concise. You will usually be able to express it to another person in one, two or at most three sentences.

This is an important characteristic to keep in mind for this type of soul communication. When you express what you have received, it can be very concise. However, that does not mean that the total teaching is limited. Very often you will be able to give teaching of great length connected with any insight you receive through direct knowing. You receive it in its essence, its condensed form. However, when you express it, you usually have to give a fuller explanation to enable others to understand.

Few people use direct knowing as their usual form of soul communication. Some people receive insights on occasion. Others have not moved to this level of soul communication. It is not important which group you are in. What is important is to appreciate this form of soul communication and to understand its significance and benefits.

This direct, clear, concise communication of the essence of teaching and wisdom is a very special treasure from the Divine. You need to have a high soul standing and frequency to receive this kind of communication. Direct knowing transforms your soul journey at a very rapid rate. It makes it possible for you to offer powerful service to others. You can state very simply what your knowing is. Very often, people will ask you to give a more complete explanation. Their response most often is one of amazement. It triggers an "ah-ha" response; however, it is quite different from the response you had when you received the insight.

Sharing what you receive is a high form of service. Giving fuller explanations of the meaning of the insight is an important teaching opportunity. Often, the teaching will come in daily conversation. The more you receive soul communication through direct knowing, the more it will become part of your daily life. It will be part of your soul journey in a significant way. You will come to discover that you receive this type of soul communication as you are teaching classes, workshops or conferences.

Direct knowing is a special quality and ability. It is a very special level of soul communication. It is almost as though you are continually receiving jewels from the Divine and the Soul World. These precious teachings that you receive are meant to be passed along. The more you pass along the insights you receive, the more you will be able to receive even more extraordinary insights and the more your soul communication ability will improve.

I have already given a teaching on the role of service. It is important to remember that teaching at this point. Sometimes people on the spiritual journey think they are special because they have received this type of soul communication and moved to the level of *knowing.* They are special, but this means they are to serve even more. That is the meaning of "special." It does not mean they are better than anyone else. It only means they give greater service because they live a higher quality of total GOLD.

Each form of soul communication that I have described in this section is a special gift from the Divine. It is important that you appreciate and value the soul communication ability that you have. Avoid making comparisons. I have given a teaching on that already. Making comparisons can create blockages in your soul journey very rapidly. It can slow down your ability to do soul communication. It can lower your accuracy. Each form of soul communication is important. Each form contributes to your own soul journey and the soul journey of others. Receive each form with absolute gratitude and devotion. Have no attachment to any one ability.

If you are just beginning to open your soul communication channels, have no expectation. Have no attachment. It is a big mistake to say, "I want to have direct knowing. I am going to work on that." Begin the way that I have described in this chapter. Go through the process the way the Divine has presented it to us. This is following nature's way. Go step by step. Be completely grateful for each step. Each channel is an incredible honor and privilege. No matter what form of soul communication you use, to think that you can communicate with the Divine in this way is truly beyond words. We are very blessed.

❖ ❖ ❖ ❖

I will now serve your spiritual journey by offering you a blessing from my soul to open your spiritual channels. Say: *Dear soul, mind and body of Master Sha, can you please offer me a blessing to widely open my spiritual channels? I am honored and appreciative. Thank you.* Then chant *Master Sha, Master Sha, Master Sha, Master Sha* continually for three to five minutes. My soul will offer you a blessing to purify your spiritual channels, increase your frequency and uplift your soul.

I offer this service to all of humanity and souls in the universe. I offer this service unconditionally to each of you. This practical exercise can be applied every day for as long as you wish to practice. The more you chant, the more blessings my soul will offer you. I serve you from the bottom of my heart.

Thank you. Thank you. Thank you.

Notes

[14] One Hand Near, One Hand Far is a basic Body Power technique of Soul Mind Body Medicine. See *Soul Mind Body Medicine*, pp.176–177. If you have headaches, hypertension, glaucoma, a brain tumor, brain cancer, Alzheimer's, or are recovering from a stroke, do not practice any Third Eye exercises, because these illnesses involve energy blockages in the brain.

[15] *Soul Mind Body Medicine*, pp. 104–108.

[16] Chinese for Shakyamuni Buddha or Gautama Buddha, the founder of Buddhism.

Soul Communication
Helps the Spiritual Journey

I have given some teachings on this already. In this chapter, I will give you further teachings and clarification with specific details and examples. This will help you deepen your understanding of how soul communication helps the spiritual journey. Keep in the mind that when I use the term "soul communication," it includes Third Eye images, Soul Language and translation, direct soul communication and direct knowing. If I am speaking about a particular form of soul communication, I will identify that form. Realize that even when I identify a particular form, the soul communication can take place in any of the other ways as well. Sometimes, I will identify a particular method of soul communication simply to give you a clearer, more concrete idea. It is not meant to limit your understanding or use of soul communication.

By now, you should understand that there are very few limits in my teachings. The only real limits are those determined by *ling fa*, spiritual law. When it comes to soul communication I shared quite clearly in Chapter 1 those questions that are not appropriate to ask according to *ling fa*. I have also been very clear about the limitations on using soul communication for others. You do not need to be concerned that you will be breaking *ling fa* and not know it. My examples and teachings give you a complete idea.

Communicating with the Divine

You might think that you have a very good idea of how to communicate with the Divine. I have already given you some examples of questions to assist you in communicating with the Divine to help your spiritual journey. Let us begin here at a basic, fundamental stage of soul communication.

At this basic stage, the question to ask is simply: *Dear Divine, what is it you want me to know?* Almost universally, the Divine wants you to know how loved you are. Now, you may very well be thinking, "Of course, I know that." That is only partly true. Most people know *intellectually* that we are loved by the Divine. Their minds have taken hold of this teaching and they can repeat it with ease. However, knowing this statement intellectually is very different from knowing it in your heart and soul. This is the difference between knowing in your mind and knowing from experience.

The teachings in this section will introduce you to ways you can know this statement in your heart and soul, and ways that you can know it from your experience. This is a precious treasure. People worldwide want to know they are loved by the Divine. Throughout history people have wanted to know and experience this reality. People have made great efforts to achieve this experience, and some have succeeded. These teachings make it possible for you and for anyone to succeed. You have the tools and the methods to receive teachings from the Divine on a daily basis. You can connect with this experience simply by asking: *What is it you want me to know?*

When you begin doing soul communication with this question, allow yourself to experience all of the emotions that accompany the responses you receive. Do not be embarrassed, shy or frightened by the responses. Very often, people are moved to tears by the Divine's response. Sometimes, people will sob uncontrollably. That is quite wonderful. Allow yourself to do this. When you are moved to tears, a release is taking place. The Divine has touched a part of your soul, heart, mind and emotions that is very tender and sometimes very painful. When you are moved to tears, that pain is soothed. It is healed. It is transformed, and this happens with great gentleness and compassion.

Some people recognize the Divine's response as their heart's desire and their soul's desire. Some people are amazed by the tenderness and devotion of the Divine. Some are overwhelmed by the realization that the Divine truly does care for each one with divine intimacy and tenderness. This quality of intimacy, tenderness, compassion and gentleness is also very intense, but it is not overwhelming. It is an intensity that is soft and caring. It does not move us faster than we are able to go.

The Divine wants us all to know in our hearts, souls and experience that we are deeply loved. This is not a new message for most people to hear, but it will be a new message for most people to live. Most people live on guard, in a state of self-protection. This stems from the belief that they must be in control. This is such an illusion! It could not be farther from the truth. The only thing that happens when one attempts to be in control is that one becomes very rigid. One becomes very set in mindsets, attitudes and beliefs. Certain attachments become "sacred" and actually replace the Divine.

The truth is that we are not in control. We simply offer our total GOLD. We respond with complete devotion. We respond with a faithful heart and a listening heart. When we do this, we experience amazing freedom. We realize that our efforts to control our own lives and circumstances, not to mention the lives of others, lead only to stress and draining of our energy. As soon as we release the illusion of control, we have made a huge step toward the experience of divine love.

It is sad that the very thing that people do to try to bring harmony, order and light to their lives does just the opposite. By trying to organize and control everything, an invisible wall is built around one's heart, effectively keeping the Divine at a distance. How can you release this control? It is easy to answer this question. Do soul communication and ask that very question. The answer will be a bit different for each of you. Every person's mindsets, attitudes, beliefs, story and soul journey manifest in different ways. So how everyone releases control will also manifest in different ways. You will receive the answer that is appropriate for you when you ask: *How can I release control? Please give me the healing blessings I need. Help me to practice what I need to release control.*

It takes trust to do this. Remember what I said earlier. If you ask a question, be ready to act on the response. If you are not willing to act on the response, do not ask the question. If you do not use the answer you are given, the Soul World will be less inclined to answer your next question. You have not shown gratitude. You have not shown respect and reverence. This is a very important principle to keep in your awareness. If you are not willing to act on the answer, do not ask the question. Once you do ask the question, follow the suggestions in the answer.

Releasing control always includes the need to trust. You might ask, "How do I trust?" As always, I could say, "Do soul communication." However, the answer will be the same for almost everyone. *The way you learn to trust is by trusting.* It is like learning to ride a bicycle. You get on the bicycle and practice. You did not go to school to learn how to ride a bicycle. You did not go to the Internet to research various resources for learning how to ride a bicycle. Your parents did not take you to workshops to learn how to ride a bicycle. You just started to do it.

You do the same thing to learn how to trust. You make a decision and then you practice. You will have many opportunities to practice. Doubts will appear. Fear will appear. Thoughts that this spiritual path is ridiculous will appear. All of these challenges will appear. When one of them presents itself, you simply make the decision to trust. You simply say, "Thank you for your appearance. I will invite you to transform to light. I have made the decision to trust." It is that simple.

The more you practice, the easier trust becomes. Very soon you will trust without going through this process of preparation and practice. Trust will be part of your being. When you were learning how to ride a bicycle, one day you got on your bicycle and rode it without any problem. This day followed many days of practice, practice and more practice. There were days when you fell and injured yourself. But from one magical day forward, you were an expert at riding your bicycle. The same will happen for trust. When you make the decision to trust, invite all of the challenges to transform to light. Tell them you have made the decision to trust. Little by little you will become quite good — even expert — at trusting.

Trust is a precious secret for the soul journey. It is a precious secret for doing soul communication. Every aspect of your soul journey is touched by this quality. Trust strengthens your total GOLD. It helps you be an unconditional universal servant. It accelerates your ability to improve the accuracy of your soul communication. Trust is important for each one of the methods of doing soul communication. It is absolutely essential for releasing control. The moment you decide to trust is a breakthrough in your soul journey. Treasure that moment. Mark it on your calendar, for it is a special birthday.

When you make this decision, you have taken the first step through the doorway to experience divine love. You will know in your heart and soul how deeply loved you are. Once you walk through the doorway, the journey continues. Once you walk through the doorway, it is almost impossible to turn your back on divine love. It becomes more important to you than the air you breathe. It is your very essence. It becomes your very existence.

This journey to divine love begins in such a simple way. You walk through the door by trusting. You enter into an experience that is a precious treasure. You enter into a privileged aspect of the Divine's heart. You are allowed to dwell in this sacred space. What an honor and privilege. In times of testing, repeating *I dwell in the heart of the Divine* is an excellent mantra to assist you in your purification and through your testing. This is the place reserved for you by the Divine. This is the message the Divine wants you to know in your heart and soul. This is what the Divine wants you to experience and to have as your heartbeat. This is how loved we are.

Recall that when the Divine gave the Universal Law of Universal Service, the first thing the Divine said was, "I am a Universal Servant." The first quality of universal service is unconditional universal love. So, realize that the first thing the Divine wants to offer to you is unconditional universal love. It is the desire of the Divine that you respond to this offering with "thank you" and that you accept and allow yourself to be embraced by this love.

This love transforms. This love removes all obstacles and melts all blockages. It does this on every level of your being, not just the spiritual level. When you accept this treasure and allow it to become your very heartbeat and breath, you are then able to manifest this divine love for others. You are able to be an unconditional universal servant to a most extraordinary degree. Your very presence can be a gift of transformation. You become the manifestation of divine light and love. This is a very special privilege and honor.

When you do soul communication, you are connecting with all of these teachings on this desire of the Divine's heart. This is a gift the Divine makes available and offers to us every day. I have given the teachings that will make it possible for you to accept and to live this gift. When you first experience the depth of divine love, you will likely be moved to tears. As I said before, allow yourself to cry. It is quite all right. In fact, it is a good thing. You are releasing what you need to release. This is a healing for you. When the tears flow with abundance, invite the source of the tears to be transformed to light, and to join you on this journey of divine love. You do not want to spend weeks, months and years in tears.

Everything is a process. As you enter deeper and deeper into the experience of divine love, you will be less inclined to cry. Rather, you will respond with deep joy and inner peace. Do not have any expectations. Allow the process to unfold. Follow nature's way. The more soul communication messages of divine love you receive, the more quickly you will move to the experience of deep joy and inner peace.

Your decision to trust and enter through the doorway of divine love is the beginning of your journey to deep joy and inner peace. I am not promising that the rest of your life will be one of joy and peace in every aspect. What I am saying is that the core of your being will experience a deep joy and inner peace that will radiate regardless of what else is going on in your life. You may experience huge ups and downs. You may be confronted by huge problems. You may have great sorrow. You may have other challenges. However, through all of the challenges of life, you will have this treasure of joy and peace because you have entered into the experience of being loved by the Divine. There is no greater gift. There is no greater treasure.

The Divine loves all humanity and all souls collectively. It is equally true that the Divine loves humanity and all souls individually. Each one is known to the Divine. Your experience of being loved by the Divine is your individual experience. It leads to total GOLD. What else can the response be? When you experience how deeply loved you are, your heart and soul have complete gratitude, obedience, loyalty and devotion. Why would your mind have any other response? This can be the only appropriate response. It makes unconditional universal service an integral part of your daily life.

When you do soul communication to ask the Divine for the message for yourself, you will very often receive messages such as the ones I have described. If you do not receive those messages, do not be concerned. The message you receive is absolutely another gift from the Divine. Each one receives the message needed at the moment.

Remember that the first universal quality is unconditional universal love. This is the very first gift given to each one by the Divine. If you receive another message, be very grateful. Know that you have already started your journey. Know that each message from the Divine to you is tailor-made for you. Each message is specific to your soul journey and soul standing. The Divine wants what is best for you and for every soul. That may not match what you think you want to hear. That would be a mindset, attitude, belief or attachment. It may also be an example of a need to control. All of these must be released. They will blur the communication you receive. It is like static on the telephone. It is difficult to hear the message with a lot of static. It is also difficult to hear the message clearly with a lot of mindsets, attitudes, beliefs and attachments. The more you can release, the clearer the line will be and the more profound the communication will be.

Communicating with the Divine is not only a privilege and honor, it is an extraordinary opportunity. Millions of people want to accelerate their soul journey. They want to increase their soul standing. They want a closer connection with the Divine. All of these desires can be achieved by using soul communication. They are the purpose of soul communication with the Divine. It is beyond words to realize that the Divine really wants to serve us in this way. It is a powerful teaching on the Divine as an unconditional universal servant.

The communication you receive can come in any and all of the forms I described in the previous chapter. Use each form of soul communication. You can receive direct teachings through direct flow. You can receive teachings through Soul Language and translation. You can receive teachings through Third Eye images. You can receive a direct knowing of the teachings. It can be mutually supportive to use various forms of soul communication. It is also good practice that helps you to continue to open your spiritual communication channels.

As you do your soul communication, you are in an extraordinarily high frequency. The light is also extraordinary. Using different forms of communication will allow you to receive the blessings of various layers of divine light and frequency associated with each form. The more blessings you receive, the more accurate you become in that form of soul communication. Your level becomes higher and higher. For this reason, it is an excellent practice to use different forms of soul communication. Each form has its own benefits.

Doing soul communication, asking guidance of the Divine and receiving the responses is also a form of service, because you will act upon the responses you receive. You will integrate the teachings into your daily life. They will become part of your being. It might take you days, weeks or months to achieve this full integration. That is all right. What is important is your desire to integrate what you received into your daily life. With this integration, you manifest the teachings you receive. The more you do this, the more obvious it will be to you. A very common way of manifesting these teachings is in your conversations. You will become aware that the messages you receive are showing up in your conversations with friends, family members and co-workers. You may not be giving a formal teaching, but you are allowing the teaching to flow through you to others. This is a great service.

Because the teachings become part of the rhythm of your daily life, you do not need to do anything special. All you need to do is speak the message when you are aware of it. There will be many occasions when a message will come to you. The message will be very clear, definite and concise. It will want to be spoken. Unfortunately, many who receive these messages are shy about speaking them. This is a pity. It is very important to move beyond this shyness. It is your privilege, honor and responsibility to share the teachings. You do not need to go into great detail. You do not need to give a long explanation. You simply need to make a statement.

When you share with others, remember to be aware of what they are asking. Respond to the question they bring you. You do not need to share every single bit of wisdom and teaching you have received. Share only the information connected with the question. The questioner can receive the teaching because he is ready for that teaching. He may not be ready for more than that at this time.

You can offer a hint that there is more. First, answer the question clearly and concisely. Then you could add, "There is more to this teaching if you are interested." If the person is ready, he will ask for more information, wisdom and healing. If the person is not ready, you have respected his level. You have not given the person more than he can handle. This is very important.

Although these teachings might be a challenge, they are not meant to be a burden. Do not become so excited and enthused that you answer a different question from the question the other person asked. Keep this in mind and your teachings will be treasures for others. The service you offer in this way will truly be universal and unconditional. You are extremely blessed when you offer service in this way.

There are many blessings on many levels that result from doing soul communication with the Divine. Obviously, transformation in your life is the top benefit. How does this happen? Doing soul communication with the Divine is somewhat like entering Heaven. The more often you enter, the more you experience this level of frequency and vibration. In turn, you are able to manifest this to those around you more and more. You literally become a blessing for yourself and others. Doing soul communication really means that you are in the unique presence of the Divine. You are participating in heavenly existence. You are able to bring this quality of light, frequency and vibration not only to those around you, but also to all humanity.

Very often people wonder what Heaven is like. When you do soul communication with the Divine, you experience an aspect of heavenly presence. You share with others through your very presence. This is not something you would share directly in conversation with many others, although there may be some who would appreciate such comments. It does not matter. It is enough for you to realize that this is another aspect of soul communication with the Divine.

It is truly a profound experience to enter into heavenly presence, to be transformed by this, and then to make it present on Mother Earth and beyond. At this particular time in the history of Mother Earth, there is a great need for Heaven and everything associated with it. When you are aware of this aspect of your soul communication, you can bring this presence to Earth. It will be profoundly healing. Every level of Mother Earth's existence needs this healing. It is a great honor to be able to bring this healing.

❀ ❀ ❀ ❀

There are numerous aspects of soul communication with the Divine. I have given you an idea of its significance and benefits. You also know that this communication can be done using all of the forms that I have described. I strongly suggest that you use this powerful gift on a daily basis. Experience the transformation it will bring about in your life. Know that this transformation is not limited to you. Know that doing soul communication daily is a very high level of service. These are some of the most powerful aspects of soul communication with the Divine. They are the unique blessings received when you do this as a daily practice.

Communicating with the
Highest Saints, Guides and Healing Angels

You can, of course, do soul communication with the highest saints, and with your guides, healing angels, wisdom figures and teachers. In this section most of the teachings will be directed toward soul communication with the highest saints. However, everything I will say is also true for communicating with your guides, healing angels, wisdom figures and teachers.

When you do soul communication with the highest saints, you are connecting with those who are assisting humanity in a special way. Those who are at the highest level in Jiu Tian (the "nine layers of Heaven") are not required to return to Earth to learn lessons. They have reached the level of purification at which lessons have been learned well. It is quite different from the souls in the lower levels in Jiu Tian. These souls need to return because they have many unfinished lessons and much that needs to be purified. A saint at the highest levels of Jiu Tian may, however, be asked to return to Earth to perform service. This is not a common occurrence. Typically, a highest saint would be asked to return to Earth only once during a 15,000-year era. The saint's response is invariably, "Yes. I will do it. I am honored to serve."

It is a great honor and privilege to do soul communication with the highest saints. They include Jesus, Mary, Shi Jia Mo Ni Fuo and Ling Hui Sheng Shi, who in the previous era was known as Guan Yin. When you do soul communication with one of the highest saints, you are connecting with the teachings, the wisdom, the practices and the frequency of that saint. Doing soul communication with more than one of the highest saints gives you a connection with many different teachings, wisdom, practices and frequencies.

Ask the same question I suggested for your soul communication with the Divine: *Dear ____, what is it you want me to know?* Again, the responses will be generous. The wisdom will be profound. Each of the highest saints has his own unique teachings. The highest saints have passed their teachings to followers and disciples. The teachings are manifest in various spiritual traditions, sometimes in a pure form, sometimes not. Through direct soul communication with one of the highest saints, you receive direct, unfiltered teachings that are tailored specifically for you. They are given for your situation in your soul journey at this time.

The uniqueness of the soul communication you receive is an extraordinary quality. You may choose to do soul communication with a high saint who is familiar to you. Consequently, you may already know many teachings from this saint. You may have used these teachings in meditation. They may have been the basis for your life choices and direction. Even so, you will be amazed at the teachings you will receive through daily communication. These teachings might reinforce what you already know. If this happens, be grateful because what you already know is being taken to a much higher level. Your understanding of the teaching will develop great depth. It will become very profound. You will understand not only the teaching, but also all of the related teachings and subtle lessons that you were not aware of before.

It is like opening a gift box and, instead of finding one gift inside, finding many gifts. In fact, this is what happens whether you do soul communication with a high saint who is familiar to you or with one who is new to you. With a high saint who is familiar, your devotion gives you the possibility of receiving an abundance of wisdom and teachings. Secrets that may not be readily given to others will be revealed to you because you have shown this saint your trustworthiness and total GOLD. It is a special honor and privilege to receive more profound teachings. Do not forget to share them with others. For example, you could express the new insights and teachings you have received by saying, "I have come to a deeper understanding of the teachings on forgiveness." Those you are addressing will be open to that kind of statement, which is very important.

When you share, it will encourage the saint to give you more and more precious treasures. It will become obvious that your GOLD is becoming more pure, that your devotion is growing, that you truly are trustworthy, and that you are not keeping the teachings just for yourself. Any teaching you have received needs to be passed along in a way that is appropriate. They are not meant to be treasures that only you enjoy, review and use. They are treasures to be passed along to others in a way that is appropriate.

When you communicate with the highest saints, you are receiving their specific teachings. You are connecting with that part of the Soul World where these teachings have been taught and lived. You are connecting with all the souls who have followed these teachings. In most cases, you are in the company of thousands of souls who have lived these teachings in their daily lives. It is quite extraordinary to realize this. You are in the presence not only of the highest saint but of all these other souls as well. You are in this field of light, which is transforming. Your frequency will be brought much closer to the frequency of the highest saint. All those who have followed the teachings will assist you to integrate, implement, manifest and share them. All of the virtue of these thousands of souls will be available to you. You connect with all of this when you do soul communication with a highest saint. You are literally surrounded by saints, not just the one with whom you are communicating. Many of these souls are on a very high level. To be in their presence is a very special blessing.

You can make this connection at any time simply by using the highest saint's name as a mantra. This is a wonderful way to go through your day. It will make it easier to respond to the difficult parts of your day. When you are experiencing difficulty, just bring the highest saint to your awareness to bless the experience. This practice will make a great difference in your daily life. It will make it more possible for you to live in total GOLD. It will transform the quality of your total GOLD.

When you do soul communication with a higher saint, you can ask, "What are the special practices that you have to teach me?" You can ask, "What are the practices to pass along to humanity?" You can also ask, "What are the secrets connected with the practices you taught long ago? What is the wisdom humanity has not discovered yet?" These are all excellent questions that will give you profound teachings and transform your current practices. Your practice will become a wisdom practice.

You may continue to ask these questions many times. Every practice is connected to layers and layers of wisdom. Every practice has wisdom that has not yet been revealed, including particular wisdom for the Soul Light Era. The wisdom of the practice will give you wonderful insights and inspirations. It will assist you in your process of transformation. You can share these teachings with others. Humanity is just beginning to connect with the profound wisdom of ancient practices. The wisdom is of such great depth that humanity has just begun to appreciate the depth. Also, it is time in the Soul Light Era to reveal other aspects of the wisdom. This is the proper time to share secrets that humanity was not ready for in previous eras.

Living in the Soul Light Era means that we have the privileged role of receiving secrets that are connected directly to the soul. Because we are at the very beginning of this era, the secrets we are receiving now are the ones needed for humanity for the time of transition into this new era. It is our role, responsibility, privilege and honor to receive these sacred and secret teachings and to pass them to others.

Asking for these new teachings is a very useful soul communication practice. You can ask similar questions for healing. Many of you will recognize a great similarity in the new teachings connected to healing and what you have studied in Soul Mind Body Medicine. Some of you will recognize the new teachings in your soul. They will feel familiar. This is because many of you have been healers in past lifetimes. You will be able to implement the new teachings immediately.

Each of the highest saints has a particular approach to healing. The responses you receive are unique to that saint. If you ask questions that are very general, you will receive teachings that are also very general. If you want to know the specific healing wisdom of a particular saint, ask. If you want specific teachings, ask specific questions. Remember the old saying: Be careful what you ask for because that is what you will get. In this case there is no need to be careful; you just need to remember that what you ask for is what you will get.

Knowing the wisdom connected with the healing makes it possible for you to benefit more and more from the healing practices. Those whom you are healing will benefit more and more. Because each of the highest saints has unique blessings and gifts, communicating with more than one of the highest saints is a very good practice. You may have a particular devotion to one or another of these saints. Continue that devotion. It is very important. Respect that devotion, but do not limit yourself. The entire Soul World is available to you. To stay with one particular high saint is limiting. Do not worry about offending that saint. In the Soul World, all of the highest saints are friends, brothers and sisters. They are not upset if you communicate with others. Quite the contrary, they are delighted that you are connecting with more and more of the Soul World and gaining a great variety of teachings, healings and blessings. Each connection that you make and each soul communication that you do increase your frequency and vibration. They increase in harmony with the saint with whom you are communicating. You connect with the virtue of all who have followed the teachings of that saint.

A word of caution: Some people get so enthused that they decide to connect with every single high saint they can possibly think of. This is overdoing it. Connect with some of the highest saints. There is no way you can connect with all of them. If you are able to do soul communication with two, three or four, that is excellent. That is a wonderful practice. It will remove the limits of communicating with just one of the highest saints, but it will keep things reasonable. You will approach your soul communication with great reverence and respect. You will avoid treating soul communication like a smorgasbord. A smorgasbord approach lacks depth. You cannot possibly receive profound teachings from dozens of highest saints.

Keep my caution in mind and try to stay with two, three or four of the highest saints. This will give you a beautiful and rich set of responses. You will be amazed at the differences in the communications you receive. There will most certainly be similarities in some teachings. All of the highest saints will at some time teach about the necessity to live in unconditional love, unconditional forgiveness and universal service. All of the universal truths will be part of their teachings. However, each one of the highest saints will approach these teachings from his own perspective. It is like looking at a picture from many different angles. You are looking at the same picture; however, you see something slightly different from every angle. When you ask the highest saints the same question, you might receive the same answer, the same wisdom, but it will be presented in a different way. Each response makes it possible for you to live the teaching in your daily life. Each response completes your understanding. Each response gives depth so you can use what you have learned. Each response reinforces the others.

Reinforcement is important for any teaching. This happens when you ask several of the highest saints the same question. Each highest saint has the opportunity to reinforce the others. Each also has the opportunity to express it according to his specific connection with the Divine. This is what each saint is passing along to you. You receive this special gift from each one. The variety of responses helps you reach a more complete understanding. It helps you develop a greater connection with the way the teachings can be used for humanity and Mother Earth at this time.

I cannot emphasize enough how important it is to connect with at least two of the highest saints and to do so on a daily basis. Everything that I have said about the highest saints is also true for your guides. As you communicate with the highest saints, guides, healing angels and wisdom figures, you will often receive messages of gratitude. They will thank you for your devotion, commitment and service. For many, this is a heart-touching experience. People are often moved to tears. It is a similar to being told by the Divine how much you are loved. When you receive messages of gratitude from a high saint whose teachings you have followed, it is very special. It is heart-touching. It can be hard to believe that the highest saints, guides, angels and wisdom figures would want to thank us.

What we can learn from this experience is that the way the saints see us is very different from the way we see ourselves. We often see only our problems and shortcomings. When the highest saints and all those in the highest realms of the Soul World look at us, they see our beauty and light. They see our commitment and devotion. That does not mean the blockages are not visible to them. It simply means their focus is on the light. This is where they connect with you and where they give you their attention. If you have lived a life of devotion and have been on the spiritual journey, there is likely a lot of light in your soul journey. When those in the Soul World look upon your soul journey, they see this magnificent light. That is why they thank you.

Those in the highest realms of the Soul World have lived a life of total GOLD. Expressing total gratitude to the Divine develops a mindset and an attitude of gratitude. As you become total GOLD, your mindsets, attitudes and beliefs shift. Little by little, they become mindsets, attitudes and beliefs of total gratitude, obedience, loyalty and devotion. Those on the highest level of Jiu Tian have expressed and manifested their total gratitude for hundreds and thousands of lifetimes. They have developed wonderful mindsets and attitudes of total gratitude. This helps us further understand why they express their gratitude to us. Gratitude is what they have become. Light is their focus.

Even if your soul journey has only a small amount of light, the highest saints and all those in the highest levels of the Soul World will place their attention there. This is a special blessing for all of us because when they place their attention on our light, they are blessing that part of our soul journey. They are increasing our light. They are improving the frequency and quality of our light. Their expressions of gratitude transform every aspect of our being.

When the highest saints express their gratitude, they let us know that our devotion, commitment, service and total GOLD are special treasures that have been observed and blessed by the Soul World. These qualities have increased our soul standing. Not only have they benefited us, they benefit all humanity, Mother Earth and beyond. The highest saints want each of us to know that the efforts we make are important and treasured. When they observe our actions, they pay attention to our efforts, our commitment and our heart's desire.

Typically, we focus on our results. If the results are not outstanding, we can feel that we have failed. We feel that there is very little light in that particular project or activity. The response of the highest saints is very different. They look at our activities, but they also see our efforts, mindsets and attitudes. These are the things that receive their attention. When all of these things are filled with light, the highest saints see our light. If any one of them is blocked, the highest saints see the blockage. The nature of the blockage will be different for each person. However, certain blockages are common. The most common blockage is ego. When the highest saints notice manifestations of ego in our actions or attitudes, they will assist in the purification process. If we respond with gratitude, the blessings we receive will be extraordinary.

When we perform our tasks, the results might be wonderful. We might be quite pleased. Once again, however, this is not what is most important to the highest saints. They are more interested in our response. Did we get a big ego from our results or did we take the opportunity to thank the Divine, our guides and all of the Soul World? Did we seize the opportunity to offer further service? The Soul World connects with what is most important for our soul journeys.

The Soul World's messages of gratitude are very tender. They will often remind you that you have been a student or disciple for many lifetimes. Some of those lifetimes may be brought to your awareness through Third Eye images. You might ask directly for information about those lifetimes, through Soul Language and translation or through direct flow. For some of you it can be very helpful to know about these past lifetimes. Others of you will not have a desire for this information. Either way is fine. What is important is to enter into the experience of the gratitude that is being given to you. Learn to receive and accept this gratitude.

It may surprise you to know that difficulties accepting gratitude are actually due to ego. As you receive messages from the highest saints, you will have many opportunities to purify your ego. Receiving and accepting their gratitude is absolutely one of the best teachers. It is an excellent way to purify at an accelerated pace. This may seem strange to you. However, people are very accustomed to being the ones to provide assistance to others and to extend their gratitude to others. When this process is reversed, they feel a bit uncomfortable. This discomfort can actually be very beneficial. It helps you release many issues you have become attached to. It helps you release many mindsets, attitudes and beliefs. It is amazing to realize that gratitude is such a powerful quality. It purifies when you extend your gratitude to others. It purifies when you receive and accept gratitude and blessings from others. Gratitude builds upon itself. It makes it possible to live more and more in the condition of gratitude. This will advance your journey more and more to the light. This is a wonderful gift that the Divine has given humanity.

Receiving and accepting gratitude requires you to enter into the condition of gratitude. As you do this, you will be better able to express gratitude toward others and to receive gratitude that is extended to you. What a delightful process! It is similar to the quality of forgiveness. We must be able to give gratitude. We must be able to receive it. Both are important. One without the other is incomplete. One without the other allows the ego to continue to grow.

Another aspect of gratitude is its connection with generosity. In order to truly be generous, it is absolutely necessary to accept gratitude from others. You cannot say, "No, thank you," or, "No, no, it was really nothing," or, "Please don't thank me." These statements are simply not possible for a person who is truly grateful. This might be surprising to some. However, when you stop to think about it, it is quite easy to see how true this statement is.

Another aspect of receiving and accepting gratitude is that this practice allows you to realize that your commitment and devotion have truly been a gift to you. When people thank you, it is important to acknowledge it. It is also important to acknowledge that all you have done has been a gift to you from the Divine. Your commitment, your devotion and your service have come from you. However, they have also come from the blessings you have received. To receive gratitude allows you to express gratitude to the Divine. It is a wonderful feedback spiral. The highest saints express their gratitude to you. You receive and accept it. As you do, you express your gratitude to the Divine. The quality of gratitude is multiplied. You are accepting gratitude and giving gratitude at the same time. It is a wonderful privilege to be able to do this. When the highest saints express their gratitude and appreciation to us, they are giving us priceless opportunities to increase our soul standing, to offer service to all humanity, Mother Earth and beyond, and to manifest a higher frequency of light. The benefits of this practice are many and great.

Receiving and accepting the gratitude of the highest saints transforms every aspect of your being. It accelerates your soul journey. It accelerates your release of mindsets, attitudes, beliefs and attachments. It is the first aspect of total GOLD. The highest saints give teachings, healings and blessings in many different ways. No matter how their communication is expressed, there will almost always be an element of gratitude. Always remember that the gratitude will be for your devotion, commitment and service. If it goes beyond that, if you get messages about how great you are, what a unique role you have, how much better you are than others, you are not receiving accurate communication. The highest saints will most definitely communicate their gratitude. They will not communicate teachings that feed your ego. Such messages are either inaccurate or simply false. Do not let this concern you. Respond as always, "Thank you for the message." Let the message know it does not match universal service. Invite it to transform to light and to be a universal servant.

The best healing for a big ego is to be an unconditional universal servant. Use my teachings to redirect the energy of messages that appeal to your ego. Do not fall into the trap of ego. It is quite easy if you remain conscious that these messages are not accurate. You can avoid many problems by following the simple suggestion of saying "thank you," inviting the message to transform to light and to join you as an unconditional universal servant. The message will also be grateful. As I have said before, every soul in the universe desires to be a universal servant. With this practice, you are assisting the soul of the message. This is great service with abundant blessings.

Follow these teachings to accelerate your soul journey, increase your soul standing, and magnify the light that is present on Mother Earth. At this time in the story of Mother Earth, these qualities and this light are urgently needed. It is truly an honor and privilege to be able to assist in this way.

Communicating with Others

Soul communication can be used with the Divine and with the highest saints. It can also used with those in other universes. We are familiar with many of the highest saints connected with Mother Earth. However, there are countless universes. There are countless heavenly realms. There are countless highest saints, guides, angels and wisdom figures. It is possible to receive soul communication from any universe and from any of the heavenly realms in that universe. You can also receive communication from beings in any universe. This is extraordinary. The possibilities are profound. If you know the names of various universes, you can speak directly to the souls in those universes. If you do not know specific names, you can simply ask for the highest souls in a universe to respond. You can ask the universe that is closest to us. You can ask the universe that is farthest away. You can ask the universe that is the newest or the oldest. The possibilities are without limit.

You can communicate using the same questions I suggested previously. In addition, you can ask questions such as: *What is the unique teaching of this universe? What is its history? What kind of a connection has it had with Mother Earth and our universe?* As you begin this type of soul communication, additional questions will present themselves. All you really need to do is start. For example, some have great interest in the lost continent of Atlantis. Ask questions of the soul of this continent. *What are your teachings? What unique gifts do you have for Mother Earth at this time? What special teachings do you have at this time?* The lost continent of Atlantis could have a great deal to communicate that would serve humanity, Mother Earth and beyond.

When you communicate with these souls, you will receive extraordinary wisdom. You will receive powerful teachings and suggestions. You might not teach this wisdom publicly. In fact, it would be wise to keep this information to yourself until there is an appropriate time to share it with others. However, everything you receive will become part of your daily life and activities. You will teach through your actions. This is a powerful way of teaching and powerful service.

When you do soul communication with other universes, you are connecting with very high level souls. The term "holy beings" would be accurate. This also lets the other universes know what level of being you wish to communicate with. You could ask: *Dear highest level holy beings, what is your special teaching at this time? You might ask: What is the teaching for me? What is the teaching for Mother Earth?*

Many secrets are waiting to be revealed to humanity. Many practices will be very helpful to humanity at this time. Many messages will assist humanity and Mother Earth during this time of transition. You can ask for those messages. You can be a special connection for Mother Earth with other universes. When your soul communication channels are very open, you have the gift of receiving immediate answers to your questions. This gift is available to everyone. What an amazing possibility! The immediacy of the response in soul communication is unique. This is quite different from standard approaches. You don't have to go to the library, find the relevant books, and study them for hours or days, even months and years. As soon as you ask your question, the response has already been initiated.

Every form of soul communication is useful for communicating with other universes and other holy beings. You may be surprised at your Third Eye images. Ask to receive more images, so that you can grow in your understanding and your ability to share what you receive.

Many of you will choose to make your first such connection through Soul Language because it is such a pure form of communication. Whatever form of communication you choose, you will receive profound teachings, wisdom and blessings. The holy beings in other universes will let you know what should be shared and what needs to wait. Pay close attention to these messages. Do not get carried away by your enthusiasm and the experience of communicating with holy beings from other universes. If you receive communication that says wait, then you must wait. If you do not follow the guidance, you are breaking *ling fa,* spiritual law. This big mistake can cause you many problems. Avoid those problems. Always pass along teachings at the appropriate time. As I said previously, if you give information that others are not ready to receive, it can slow their soul journey. This is not good service.

The holy beings in other universes have many special gifts, blessings and teachings for those who do soul communication with them. At the appropriate time, those teachings will be shared with all humanity and Mother Earth. Some teachings can be shared immediately; others will wait. Even if you cannot share certain teachings immediately, your own soul journey will benefit. The wisdom you receive will help you understand many aspects of the soul journey much better.

Keep your communications clear and filled with light. We are blessed to have this opportunity to develop the ability of soul communication to bring greater light to our own soul journey and the soul journey of others. Using this gift is a blessing for you. Using this gift is a blessing for others.

Soul Communication
for Healing

Soul communication is extremely valuable for healing. Soul com-munication assists in identifying issues that need healing. It is the vehicle for making a connection with the issue to be healed. In the Soul Light Era, everything will be done soul to soul. Communi-cating soul to soul moves the healing process to an entirely different level. The benefits are profound. Soul communication is used to re-ceive information for healing and to direct the healing process. Soul communication accelerates healing.

Third Eye

Each form of soul communication can be used for healing. Third Eye ability is particularly helpful. With this ability, you can see the blockages. This happens in several ways. One way is to see where in the body there is a blockage (accumulated energy) or where en-ergy is deficient. When you receive the image, you know whether it is a blockage or deficient energy. In almost all cases, it is a block-age because eighty-five to ninety percent of health issues are due to blockages.

When you see an area in the body with an excess of energy, you know to direct the healing blessing there. For example, if you want to use One Hand Near, One Hand Far,[17] your Third Eye images enable you to know the proper placement of your hands. It makes it possible to teach the other person where to place his hands. This is actually all the information you need from your Third Eye images.

People with a very highly developed Third Eye can see much more detail. They can see into the organ. They can see all aspects of the organ. They can see exactly where the blockage is. As they are giving a healing blessing, they can observe the movement of light and the dissipation of the blockage. Third Eye images show that the blockage has dissipated and can show how much of the blockage remains. With this information, the healer knows how to continue the healing process. This is a very helpful ability. Those who have this ability are very blessed. It helps them accelerate the healing process for themselves and others. It is also fascinating to see what is actually happening during the healing process. This will enhance one's understanding of Soul Mind Body Medicine as a self-healing technique.

If you do not have this ability, have no attachment. It is not absolutely necessary. You can be a very powerful healer without Third Eye capabilities. It is an aid to supplement the healing process. Those with a highly developed Third Eye can sometimes also see the events in a person's lives that led to the current issue. I will discuss this further later in this chapter.

A very few people have some extremely highly developed Third Eye abilities. They can see images that go beyond the organs and the location of the blockage in the organ. They can actually see at the cellular level, even down to the DNA and RNA. They can see how the DNA and RNA are transformed by a healing. It is quite amazing to know that changes occur on the cellular level and the level of DNA and RNA on a regular basis. In fact, changes take place every time one uses the soul healing techniques of Soul Mind Body Medicine. It is quite amazing to know that something so simple as One

Hand Near, One Hand Far can bring about profound changes at the level of the cells, the DNA and the RNA. The One Hand Near, One Hand Far Body Power technique is so simple even small children can benefit by using it.

Again, if you do not have highly developed Third Eye ability, do not be concerned. What you have is exactly what you need. Have no attachment or expectation that you will develop Third Eye ability. What you are given is exactly appropriate for you and your soul journey. It is the particular gift of the Divine for you at this time. Always practice total GOLD, remembering that the G stands for total gratitude. Gratitude is very important. Some will say, "I am very grateful but I wish I had greater Third Eye ability." This kind of statement says, "I am grateful but I am not grateful" at the same time. One part of this statement cancels the other. Move in the direction of total gratitude. I cannot tell you enough that it is completely possible to be a powerful healer without having high level Third Eye abilities.

You can receive Third Eye images showing you the source of the health issue. For example, a person may have a very delicate stomach. There can be many reasons for this. Past life experiences often have great influence on one's present health. Those with delicate stomachs may receive images to show what related events happened to them in past lives. They may have been poisoned. They may have had stomach injuries. Past life events are part of one's soul memories. Soul memories manifest in one's physical, mental and emotional responses to life. They affect one's soul journey. Those who have had stomach injuries will need to heal those memories to heal fully in this life.

If you see such images for another person, do not say anything. Keep your comments to the basic cause of sickness: too much energy or not enough energy. This is foundation teaching which should always be emphasized. If you see Third Eye images of past lives, it is not appropriate to share them unless the other person asks specifically for this information. If the person asks, "What is the source of my health issue?" you need to determine if he is asking about physical sources or past lives. You must answer the question he is asking.

Typically, people who ask, "What is the source of my health issue?" are asking about the root physical cause. They are not interested in past lives or any other kind of information. Give them only the information they request. Give them the information that will be useful. When they know the physical source, they can do more effective self-healing. Unless asked, do not give Third Eye images of past life events. Stay with the basic teachings of Soul Mind Body Medicine. These teachings are unique in their simplicity and effectiveness. Do not try to change any of these approaches. The Divine has given humanity soul healing tools that can be used by anyone, anywhere and at any time. Treasure these gifts. Treat them with great gratitude, respect and reverence. When you have this mindset, attitude and belief as you give healing blessings, the recipient will sense your attitude and share in your appreciation. Appreciating the uniqueness of the gifts we have been given is essential. Manifesting that appreciation is also essential. Your power will grow very quickly. You will become an amazing healer.

Those with Third Eye abilities can often see the countless saints, buddhas and holy beings who are present for every healing blessing. It will be obvious that these healing blessings are powerful because of this direct connection with the highest levels of the Soul World. It is wonderful to know you have so much help when you are giving healing blessings, whether to yourself or to others. You are literally surrounded by saints, buddhas and holy beings. This is a wonderful honor and privilege. Those who can see these images will have an added appreciation of the uniqueness and power of soul healing methods.

Those with Third Eye abilities can also see the soul of a health issue. They can see this soul's gratitude for receiving healing blessings and the soul's honor at the number of saints, buddhas and holy beings who are present to support with their blessings. In a sense, it is extraordinary to realize that countless saints are present each time a healing blessing is given. In another sense, it is not surprising at all. It is the saints' heart and soul desire to serve humanity and Mother Earth in this way. We are very grateful to them. They are also very grateful to us. The opportunity to serve is a special treasure. Every time you give or receive a healing blessing, you are offering service to the recipient. You are offering service by giving this opportunity to the entire Soul World. The blessings are multiplied more than you can imagine. The benefits for all are profound.

When you use Third Eye ability for healing, it is important to remember you are receiving images — an image of the blockage, an image of past life experiences. Everything is an image, so it is important to interpret what you receive. Some images are easy to interpret. For example, an image of blocked light represents a blockage. In contrast, images of past life experiences connected with a health issue generally need to be interpreted. Even if you are not going to give this information to the other person, the image needs clarification. Clarification comes from interpreting what you have received. This clarification and interpretation can come via other images, in direct flow or by direct knowing. However you receive the interpretation, it is important to connect with the essence of the image. This is very important for you as a healer. For your own self-healing, clarification of images helps your soul journey. It helps you release mindsets, attitudes and beliefs, reach emotional balance and, most certainly, it helps you heal. Clarification and interpretation are essential once you receive the image.

Many people who are new to Third Eye abilities stop at the image. They forget this next step. As a result, the information they receive is limited. The benefits are limited. These suggestions will help you receive the maximum benefits and offer the greatest service to others. You may share your images with others, but the interpretations will guide you in giving the healing blessings. This guidance will make you a more powerful healer. Your service will be more profound. You and those you serve will experience wonderful benefits.

Soul Language and Translation

Soul Language and translation is a special gift to humanity for many reasons. It carries great frequency and vibration. It carries great light. Soul Language and translation is a powerful and profound healing tool. I have given some examples in previous chapters. Soul Language and translation gives you wonderful information because this form of communication is very pure. Those who use it benefit greatly. Those who receive healing blessings from it also benefit greatly.

You can use Soul Language to speak to the soul of the health issue. The response that you receive will assist you in giving a healing blessing to yourself or others. Often, the information you receive from the soul of the health issue will be a surprise. You can learn what the blockage is. You can learn the root cause of the blockage. You can also learn other information about the health issue. For example, you might learn that the health issue is eager to improve. You can ask the health issue how you can best assist in the healing process. If you are healing another person, ask how that person can assist. Ask if there is anything else the soul of the health issue wants to tell you that will help in the healing process. You might think of other questions as you receive answers to the ones I have suggested. These are only suggestions. Do not limit yourself to these few ideas.

It is possible that the soul of the health issue will say that it does not want to improve. This is very important information. Go further.

Ask why. Find out if there is anything you can do to persuade the health issue to change its choice. If you are doing healings for another person, ask if there is anything the person can do so that the health issue will want to improve. You can ask what else you need to know, or what else the other person needs to know. You might learn that the health issue is connected to many other people. Find out what you need to do to begin or to accelerate the healing process.

If you are working with another person, you can ask the same questions. However, if the other person has not asked for this information, remember the basic guideline I have already given you. Only give information that has been requested. Even if you know much more, it is not appropriate to share it. The other person must be ready. If you share information with people who are not ready to receive it, you can be doing great harm, not only to their physical journey but also to their soul journey.

There are many ways you can help someone without directly telling him the additional information you have received through Soul Language. Offer the appropriate healing blessing. Teach the self-healing that is essential for ongoing healing blessings. These are essential services. The healing process has two components. Receiving healing blessings is one. The other is practicing self-healing. Both are essential. One part will not work without the other. It is like trying to ride a bicycle with one wheel. You might be able to move a bit, but it will take great effort and progress will be very limited. If you have two wheels, it is easy. You can go fast or slow. You can go wherever you want to go. Just as both wheels are needed, both components of the healing process are needed.

When you are instructing others on their self-healing needs, you may have discovered things that are important for their healing process that they have not requested to know. However, you can make a relevant suggestion. For example, you can suggest Universal Meditation. There are several in my book *Soul Mind Body Medicine*[18] that are designed for healing. It would be quite appropriate to suggest those meditations. This is as specific as you need to be. You will not give unsolicited information about people or circumstances or past life events. You can mention other meditations that are your favorites. You can mention meditations that have been helpful to others. These suggestions give the other person ways to continue the healing process that will address the information you received through Soul Language and translation or other forms of soul communication.

The situation is different if someone comes to you specifically for information about his life situation, health situation, job or whatever. If a person has come to you for this specific guidance, then it is appropriate to share the information you receive from the Soul World. This type of soul communication is also very healing. It can be considered a way of using Soul Language and translation for healing. I call it soul guidance. Soul guidance can be offered for physical health issues, mental issues, emotional issues or spiritual issues. When you do Soul Language and translation for soul guidance, you will receive very pure and refined responses. These responses will be very helpful to the person who requested guidance. Many areas of confusion and many blockages can be transformed almost immediately through this wonderful method of soul communication. It is truly an honor and a privilege to be able to use it for yourself and for others.

Besides receiving information about health issues, Soul Language itself can be used to give healing blessings. You can do this silently or out loud. Silent Soul Language vibrates the smaller cells. Vocalized Soul Language vibrates the bigger cells. Chanting Soul Language slowly is yin. Chanting rapidly is yang. When giving a healing blessing, alternate speaking your Soul Language aloud and silently so that the recipient gets the most varied and greatest possible benefits.

Because Soul Language also connects with the highest saints, those highest holy beings who have been healers throughout the ages will respond in a powerful way by joining you in the healing blessing. If you begin your healing blessing with a particular mantra and the mantra then turns into Soul Language, all the souls associated with the mantra will also come and assist. This is quite extraordinary. For those who have Third Eye abilities, it is magnificent to see.

When you use Soul Language to receive information, it is important to have an accurate translation. You can tell whether a translation is accurate in several ways. One way is your physical response. If you feel comfortable throughout your whole body, this is a sign the translation is accurate. If you have pressure on the crown chakra, this also is an indication the translation is accurate. If the translation matches other information you receive, it is accurate. Accuracy is extremely important.

I have discussed the use of Soul Language to identify health issues. You no doubt understand that translation is a vital part of the process. The accuracy of your translation will increase the more you practice. Practice on yourself first. Practice on your friends or family members.

Use Soul Language and translation for things besides healing blessings, as I have described. This too will increase your accuracy. It is like exercising different muscles in your body. The more you exercise, the stronger your entire body becomes. This is true for translating Soul Language. The more you use Soul Language and translation for a variety of purposes, the stronger and better developed your ability will be. This is a very important realization to keep in your awareness.

If you are a beginner, use Soul Language and translation at every opportunity. If you know someone who has developed this ability, ask that person to listen to your translation. Ask for suggestions. This is very helpful. It is extremely important to keep in mind that the best translations are brief and to the point. Such translations are more likely to be accurate. A translation that goes on and on has likely drifted away from a true translation. Accuracy is very important when you use Soul Language in the healing process to identify health issues and related issues. When you use Soul Language to offer a healing blessing, translation is not needed. Simply speak Soul Language and enjoy it.

Your Soul Language can change for different healing blessings. There may be a particular Soul Language connected with each organ, with each system and with each health issue. This makes perfect sense. Every organ, system and issue has a soul. The soul of the liver is quite different from the soul of the stomach. That means the Soul Language for the liver will be quite different from the Soul Language for the stomach. This is true for all of the organs, systems and health issues.

It is always important to remain flexible. What I have just described does not necessarily apply to every single person who uses Soul Language. Your Soul Language could be very similar for each organ, system and health issue. Avoid having set ideas. Do not box yourself in with expectations. I have described what usually happens, not what always happens. If it does not happen for you, that is quite all right. Whatever you receive is a blessing and a very pure form of connection with the Soul World. Whatever you receive is appropriate for you and the healing blessings you are giving.

Do not compare yourself to others. As I taught in an earlier chapter, comparisons are actually a subtle form of complaining. Avoid complaining, especially when you are trying to give a healing blessing. When you are giving a healing blessing, it is necessary to be a pure channel for divine light and love. If your mind is busy with comparisons, it will be difficult to be a pure channel. This is another reason to avoid making comparisons.

When you use Soul Language to give healing blessings, you multiply the benefits the person receives. You are connected to the Soul World in a very special and very pure way. Use the mantra San San Jiu Liu Ba Yao Wu before you begin the Soul Language. Using this mantra connects you with Master Guo, with Pu Ti Lao Zu[19] and with all the highest saints in the Soul World who are connected with Master Guo and Pu Ti Lao Zu. It connects you with all who have used this mantra. It connects you with the soul of this mantra. All of these connections bring great virtue. All of this virtue is directed toward the issue that needs the healing blessing.

Any mantra you use will have similar connections. Whatever mantra you choose to use, I suggest that you begin with San San Jiu Liu Ba Yao Wu. This is the mantra for soul communication. It will help connect the health issue to the souls of all those who will give healing blessings. This is a very powerful connection.

You can communicate through Soul Language with some of the high saints who are assisting in the healing blessing. Ask to connect with their Soul Language. Then, ask them through Soul Language how they are assisting. You will receive extraordinary teachings. Each one of the highest saints has a unique gift and contribution to the healing process. When you translate their teaching, you will learn many valuable lessons regarding techniques for offering healing blessings. You will receive insights and wisdom that you would not have been able to figure out.

For example, the emotion connected with the stomach is stress, so you could ask for a teaching on how stress affects the stomach. You could ask for teachings on how a lack of balance in stomach energy affects stress. There are countless questions that you can ask. Asking this type of question will give you great wisdom and wonderful insights. Besides asking for approaches to healing for particular health issues, you can also ask for the wisdom connected with an issue. How does each issue connect with the person's soul journey?

This last question is the essence of real wisdom. When you ask this question, you are on the road to transformation. When your clients are willing to ask this question, they are also on the road to transformation. It is a great honor and a great privilege to be able to ask these questions and to pass the answers along to others.

If you are experiencing emotional imbalance, you can speak to the soul of your Message Center. Ask some of the questions I have suggested before. You can also speak directly to the soul of the emotion. Ask what is needed. Ask how you can heal the root cause of the emotional imbalance. If the emotion is one that you know is directly connected with an organ, ask how you can give healing blessings to that organ. Ask what the connection is between the emotion and the organ. Each situation will be a little different. For some, there will be a weakness in the organ. For others, there will be an excess of the emotion. Besides giving healing blessings to the organ, ask what it is in your mindset, attitudes and beliefs that triggers a particular emotional response. Ask what it is that needs to be transformed. Then, offer healing blessings to bring about the transformation.

There are many other questions that you can ask through Soul Language and translation to bring healing to the emotions and to the organs. Being able to use Soul Language and translation is a wonderful gift and brings many blessings in the healing process.

You can also ask the soul of the health issue: "What is it that you need to heal rapidly?" You will be surprised by the answers that you receive. You can ask what changes you need to make to accelerate your healing process. These changes would be in mindsets, attitudes, beliefs and behaviors. If you truly want to accelerate your healing process, this is a very important question to ask. Ask the soul of the health issue.

Once again, make sure you really want to know the answer before you ask the question. Once you have the answer, it is vital to put it into practice. To ask a question of the Soul World and then ignore the answer is very foolish. It is like inviting someone to your home and then ignoring them. It is much better not to ask the question at all. Because what you receive in Soul Language is very pure information, it is very powerful. This is why it can accelerate your healing process *if you use the information.* Treat the information with great respect.

You are receiving teachings that humanity has not accessed before. You are offering an extraordinary service to yourself, to your clients and to all humanity. It is very important to share what you receive in your teachings with other healers. You will have profound insights about healing many common issues. Those insights will be helpful to hundreds, thousands and eventually millions of people. If you are the one to receive that information, you are very honored. You are very blessed.

Healing the Ego

The ego can appear in our lives in many different ways. Because ego is a major barrier and blockage in our soul journeys, it often manifests in physical issues. To address issues of the ego, it is best to connect with the Divine, with one of the highest saints or with your own soul. Ask any of them how to bring about healing for your ego. If you speak directly to the soul of your ego, there is a very strong possibility that you will receive false messages. Your ego wants to continue to be in charge. Your ego is quite certain that it knows best. And your ego is convinced that having control is really going to be most helpful to you. These are all dangers. They will seriously slow your healing process. To avoid these particular problems, go directly to the Soul World, to the highest saints, to the healers whom you know in the Soul World, or even to healers whom you don't know. Speak to any one of the highest saints. They have all had wonderful experiences of healing their own egos and assisting their followers to heal theirs. This is the way to approach healing the ego.

immediately. Receiving direct teachings from the Soul World on how to heal a particular issue is a marvelous treasure. Using direct soul communication can greatly accelerate the healing process.

Everything that I said about using Soul Language and translation for healing is true for direct soul communication. If a person comes to you with a request for healing, pay attention to the request. Give the healing for the request. You may silently ask what the root cause is. You may silently give a healing blessing to the root cause. If the person asks you what the root cause of the issue is, then you may share your information. If the person does not ask, then what you receive is not to be shared.

It is not always necessary to ask what the root issue is. Simply addressing the health concern and directing a healing blessing to it is fine. As the health issue improves, the root cause will also improve. Blockages will be cleared or energy will be boosted. This may be slower than addressing the root cause directly, but that is all right. The root cause will be addressed, either directly or indirectly. Either way is perfectly fine. Great benefits will be received.

When you are dealing with a chronic health issue, addressing the root cause is important. For an acute health issue, one that has just occurred recently, simply doing a healing blessing for the issue would be quite appropriate. Your approach can depend on your style. Some healers always like to go to the root cause of a health issue. For other healers, the root cause is not as important. Each approach is good. Each one brings great blessings. Each one is profound service. You may prefer to use one approach in some situations and the other approach in different situations. Direct soul communication is helpful whatever your preferred approach.

You can also communicate directly with healing angels, with your guides and with the Divine. You can ask for the most effective way of bringing healing to the health issue. Again, ask one soul. Do not ask several of them the same question. If the health issue is connected with a relationship, you can get very useful information by doing direct flows with the soul of the relationship. When a relationship is involved, very often the person will ask what the real issue is. In this case, sharing the information you receive is quite appropriate. If the person simply asks for a healing for a relationship, but does not ask the reason for the disharmony, the same general principle applies: give only the information requested.

It is difficult for many healers to avoid giving extra information in the case of relationships because they have been trained to give this information. In my teaching, using soul communication to focus on answering the question asked is of the greatest importance. Healing the situation that has been requested is extremely important. Continuing on to receive and give additional information is not helpful. In fact, it may slow down the healing process. Be sure to avoid doing this.

I do suggest that you keep a record of what you receive. You will be able to use the teaching in other situations. What you receive in direct soul communication comes through your spiritual channels. If it truly is direct communication, you will not be able to remember much of it. That is why it is important to document it. The teachings you receive are treasures. The wisdom is ancient and sacred. It is given to humanity at this time because there is a great need for it. You receive these teachings and wisdom because it is for you and for all humanity. All you need to do is take a few notes or make an audio recording of your direct flow so that you can remember the teaching you received.

If you are working with a client, you could even ask for the teachings and the most appropriate healing before the client arrives. Everything can then be recorded before you see the client. All that you receive is very important. The responses we are given at this time are precisely the ones needed. They will be needed even more as Mother Earth's purification continues and intensifies. This is another important reason to keep a record of what you receive.

When you use direct soul communication for healing, you should move into the condition of the master healer, the highest saint, the Divine or the transmission with whom you are communicating. In this condition you can be a very pure channel. You connect with the frequency and vibration of the soul giving you the teaching. You bring all of this to the healing experience. The healing will be extremely powerful. The transformation can be profound.

Entering into the condition has many layers of benefits. It also greatly increases your soul standing. When this happens, your abilities increase in turn. Giving healing blessings in the condition will be a great benefit to the recipient. It will also be a great benefit to Mother Earth, to all humanity and beyond.

These are the main ways to use direct soul communication for healing. Every situation that needs healing can benefit from direct soul communication. As you use these suggestions and teachings, you will discover many other ways. Other than the cautions I have mentioned, the only limits are those of your own imagination. The more you use direct soul communication for healing, the more possibilities you will discover. Be flexible in how you use direct soul communication. Use it often and your ability will increase. Use it often and your accuracy will increase. Use it often to serve and your soul standing will be uplifted. Use it often to more completely be an unconditional universal servant. You are blessed.

To end this chapter, I would like to give you an example of how you can use soul communication to offer a healing to others remotely. For example, if one of your dear friends who lives very far from you is sick, you can still use direct soul communication to offer a healing. First, say *hello: Dear soul, mind and body of my friend Jared, I love you. You have the power to heal yourself. Do a good job. Thank you. Dear Jared's soul, what is the appropriate healing for Jared at this time?*

You may receive a response that is very direct. You may get a message that a particular organ or system is out of balance. If you get such a message, offer a blessing directly to that organ or system. You may only receive a message that it is a spiritual blockage. In this case, offer a healing blessing for your friend's Message Center. This is how you can use soul communication to guide your healing of others and yourself.

After you have found the appropriate area for healing, you can begin the healing. In this example, if Jared had a spiritual blockage, you would say: *Dear soul, mind and body of San San Jiu Liu Ba Yao Wu, I love you. Can you offer Jared a healing blessing for his Message Center? I am very grateful. Thank you.* Then chant *San San Jiu Liu Ba Yao Wu* repeatedly for at least one minute, the longer the better. You can apply this technique to heal any aspect of the physical, emotional, mental and spiritual bodies.

The more you practice soul communication, the more service you will offer to humanity and all souls of the universe. Your soul standing will increase with each blessing and service you offer. This is the purpose of your life. You and your soul will benefit greatly. As a universal servant, you will receive flowers of virtue directly from God's heart. This is the key to your spiritual journey.

Notes

[17] This important Body Power technique is explained in *Soul Mind Body Medicine,* pp. 176–177.

[18] See *Soul Mind Body Medicine,* Chapter 5, pp. 67 ff.

[19] Pu Ti Lao Zu is one of the highest Taoist saints. He is a top leader in the Soul Light Era.

[20] As a divine channel, vehicle and servant, I have transmitted permanent divine healer souls to hundreds of people to create Soul Mind Body Medicine Soul Healers.

Soul Communication
for Teaching

Soul communication can be used for teaching. It can be used when you teach one person, a small group or a large group. How do you use soul communication for teaching? Connect with the Divine. Connect with the highest saints. Connect with the soul of your particular teaching. Connect with your guides and teachers. Connect with the souls of everyone who will listen to the teaching. Making these connections consciously is very important. When you do, you are in the condition of the teaching. What you receive will be directly connected to each of the souls you have called upon. For example, if you are teaching Soul Mind Body Medicine, connect with the soul of Soul Mind Body Medicine. If you are doing a workshop on a particular aspect of healing, such as Universal Meditation, connect with the soul of that aspect. Maintain that connection as you are doing the teaching. Maintain the connection with all the souls I have named.

When you use soul communication for teaching, you are in direct connection with the Soul World and the Soul Light Era. When you teach in this way, all you need is the topic. You do not need to do extensive research. You do not need to do extensive practice. You simply need to know the topic that you will be teaching. If you feel more comfortable making an outline, do so. However, be sure that your outline is brief and high-level. Avoid adding details. The best outline is simply:

- What is the subject?

- Why is it significant?

- What are the benefits?

- What are the practices to develop abilities and power?

That's it! You really do not need any more than that. In the following sections, I will explain how to apply each soul communication channel to doing the actual teaching.

Direct Soul Communication

I do all of my teaching in flow. That means I do all of my teaching in direct soul communication. My Assistant Teachers also teach in flow. When you teach in flow, you are in direct communication with the Divine or with the highest saints on duty. You are literally expressing their teachings. You let them "borrow your mouth." It is your voice but it is their teaching and wisdom. When I teach, in many cases I do not even have a topic before I start. I simply ask the Divine to give me the topic and provide the teachings that are needed. As soon as I open my mouth, the topic is identified and the teaching begins.

Doing your teaching in direct flow requires this quality of trust. You must be confident that the Divine will give you the topic and that the Divine will actually do the teaching on that topic for you. Do not question: *Is this truly from the Divine? Is this the correct topic? Why doesn't this topic seem to fit with the previous topics?* When you use your mind to question, you are no longer operating from the soul. You have shifted to logical thinking. You are creating obstacles to your direct flow. It is important to allow logic and direct communication to blend. However, it is most important to allow the soul to be in charge.

Other questions to definitely avoid include: *Is this a direct flow? Is it accurate? Is this all the Divine has to say?* These questions may be natural, but they will only confuse the issue and make it difficult for you to do direct flow. Any difficulties you experience in doing direct flow really come from you. They come from your mind. They come from your beliefs. They come from your attitudes. You may argue, "No, they come from my experience." Let's back up and look at that experience. How did you approach the idea of doing direct soul communication? Like many people, perhaps like most people, did you approach it with doubt and a huge question mark? Did you ask: *Is this really true? Can I really do this?* With this approach, you are immediately placing limits on your ability to do direct soul communication. The more limits you place on yourself, the more difficult it will be for you to do direct soul communication. Again, the difficulty, the root of the issue, lies with you. This is not to assign blame or make you feel guilty or depressed. This mindset is very common. It just highlights the fact that the mind and the ego are two of our biggest hurdles on the spiritual journey. I strongly encourage you to release the mindsets and attitudes that are not helpful to you. One way to do that is to trust. Trust the teaching. Trust yourself. Trust the Divine.

When you use direct communication for teaching, it is very important to keep your Message Center open throughout your teaching. You must keep the entire lecture in flow. If you waver and start to operate from your mind and conscious thought, you have lost the direct communication. You have lost the connection with the souls who are giving and guiding the teaching. You will feel different and your audience will be aware of a change in the quality of the teaching and wisdom they are receiving.

When you keep your Message Center open, you stay in the condition of the Divine. This is what makes the teaching truly divine. Staying in the condition of the Divine simply means that you are allowing the Divine to use your voice. To prepare for this, say *hello* to the Divine and ask for a topic: *Dear soul, mind and body of the Divine, can you please give me the topic that is most appropriate for my audience at this time?* If you need more than one topic, repeat this request as much as needed. Once you have received a topic, begin to speak Soul Language silently. You will be aware of a shift in your consciousness. When this happens, you can end the Soul Language and begin the teaching.

Too simple to believe? It actually is this simple. You do need to be aware of your level of accuracy, which depends on your soul standing. When you teach in flow, it is important to tell your audience that your accuracy is above average, but not one hundred percent. No one is one hundred percent accurate. That would be as accurate as the Divine, which is simply not possible.

Let your audience know further that what they hear from you must match the practical world. If it does not match, then that part of the teaching was not accurate. However, there is a great difference between identifying teachings that are not accurate and recognizing teachings that are challenging but accurate. It is natural for people to resist, ignore or eliminate the challenges in what they hear. But if one consistently ignores or eliminates challenges, progress in the soul journey is not possible. If you hear teachings that are challenging, the most appropriate response is to say, "Thank you. Thank you. Thank you," as I discussed in a previous chapter.

When you teach in flow, there are several techniques you might want to use. Before the lecture begins, ask the Divine for the most appropriate topic. Having a topic is really all you need. Once you have the topic, it is possible to flow the content right in front of your audience. When you have the topic, you will also be given the structure for your class. You may not receive it in an outline form. However, as soon as the Soul World gives you a topic, it also gives you the structure for presenting it. It gives you the examples that put the topic in the context of daily life. If you have already announced your topic, then of course you will use that topic. In this case, you can ask for more detail that will be specific to your audience. You can also ask for the main points of your lecture and write them down. Use that as a reference for your teaching. This is another way to stay connected to the teaching and wisdom of the Divine or the highest saint who is giving you the teaching.

Sometimes you may want to do even more advance preparation, such as a PowerPoint or other audiovisual presentation. Prepare it in exactly the same way — in direct soul communication. Ask for the main topic and subtopics in outline form. You will be amazed and delighted at the completeness and accuracy of the presentation you receive. The resulting presentation will be exactly what you need. This presentation will also be very helpful to your audience. They will not need to take notes. They can simply listen and receive. They can keep their Message Centers open and go into the condition of the teaching with you. This is a great blessing.

Another way to prepare to teach in flow is to talk to the souls of those who will be your audience. Ask them what is most important for them to learn. Ask them what they are most interested in. When you ask what is most important, you will get a response from their souls. *The soul journey is most important. Being an unconditional universal servant is most important.* Ask what it is they want to learn, what one or two ideas they want to take with them and use in everyday life.

When you ask these questions, what you receive in flow is what you will present. Ask these questions before your event. Some people like to do so the day before. Some people like to do so five minutes before. When you do it is up to you, but holding this type of soul conference is very helpful both for you and for your audience. If you are just beginning to teach in flow, write down the guidance you receive as a reference. If you are very experienced at teaching in flow, you do not need to write down the guidance. You will follow it automatically.

Proceed in the ways I have described. Simply look at the ideas you have received and open your mouth. The Divine and the highest saints will provide you with the teachings. They will give you the best responses to questions. Their teachings come from infinite wisdom and may include ancient sacred and secret teachings. What you will receive and give to those in your audience are treasures. As you are in the condition of the Divine and the highest saints, you will receive their messages and, in turn, teach their messages in the appropriate way to your audience.

Sometimes when people hear that they are to teach in flow, they become worried. They immediately say: *I have never done a flow. I cannot do a flow,* and so on. These statements simply are not true. You may not have done a flow before. However, you will be able to do it. The key ingredient is your own effort. For those who are willing to make the effort, great results will follow. When I talk about effort in doing a flow, I do not mean the same type of effort usually associated with completing a task, which is investing one's determination and willpower from one's own source of energy. The "effort" required to teach in flow is to remain open to the teachings of the spirit, open to receiving the messages. Your openness is the key factor.

Teaching in direct flow is an excellent way to guarantee the quality of the teaching. When teaching comes from the Divine or the highest saints, the quality is there. Simply follow the guidance of the Divine and the highest saints. As I said, they will give you the topic and also the outline, which simply means that one idea will follow from another. They will give you the details. They will give you the examples. They will give you the practices that will be needed. They will even let you know when to give your audience a break. All of this will come through your flow.

As you complete an idea, you may receive a message that the group needs to stand up and do an energy practice or that you need to give a blessing to the group to increase their energy. You may receive a message that you need to give a blessing to the group to ground them. You may get a message that the group needs to do Lower Dan Tian and Snow Mountain Area practice. All of this can be part of the flow that you receive. It is very important for you to be mindful of these messages. Often when teaching in flow, the experience of the flow becomes very profound. As your consciousness becomes strongly connected with the Divine and the highest saints, you go very deeply into their condition and the condition of the teaching. When this happens, you can miss some messages, such as one telling you that the group needs a blessing. To ensure that you do not miss such messages, you can ask the Divine or the highest saints to give you a clear signal when it is appropriate for the group to receive a blessing. All of this is part of teaching in flow.

It is very important when you are teaching in flow to keep your Message Center open. As you gain more experience teaching in this way, you may at times actually receive two flows at the same time. One flow is the teaching that is to come out of your mouth. The other flow may be some clarification that you need, or it may be a more profound teaching of the same wisdom on your frequency and level. This level of teaching would be appropriate for your soul standing, which in many cases will be higher than that of your audience. It is not to be presented to your audience. Be aware of this possibility.

The wisdom in all your flows, both the ones you speak and the ones that are simply for you to receive, is profound. It is transforming. It is healing. It is rejuvenating. It changes the soul standing of everyone who is present. It changes your soul standing in a powerful and significant way. When you teach "in the condition," your frequency and vibration are brought into greater and greater harmony with the Divine and the highest saints. When this happens, every aspect of your being is transformed. Your soul journey becomes much more a journey of light. Your virtue increases. There is healing, rejuvenation and transformation on the physical, mental and emotional levels.

After you have completed your teaching in flow, you may not remember the content. Do not be concerned about this. The content is in your Message Center. Your soul has received the teaching. When you need the wisdom, the teaching, the practice, the healing and the blessing, you have access to all of them. Often people will come up to you after or during a break in the lecture and ask you to repeat some part of the teaching. You will simply have to tell them you do not remember because you did it in flow. More than likely, there are other listeners who will be able to help the questioner. Informing your audience that you do not remember because you did the entire teaching in flow is in itself a teaching. It tells your audience that they have received something very special. They have not received something from your logical thinking, but rather something directly from the Soul World. They have received extraordinary treasures that are profound and powerful.

Teaching that is done in direct soul communication has a very high frequency and vibration. It is a powerful tool for healing, rejuvenation and transformation. It benefits the teacher and it benefits those who are listening. Doing direct flow to receive and deliver teachings is a great honor and privilege. The teacher-in-flow is the voice for the Divine and the highest saints. The teacher says, "The teachings are from the Divine. I am using only my voice." To be able to say this is a great honor.

To teach in flow is to release secrets from the universe and wisdom from the Soul World that have not been released in this way before. Teaching in flow is also a profound connection to the Soul

Light Era, an era in which everything will follow the lead of the soul. When you teach in flow, you allow your soul to be in charge. You allow the Soul World to be in charge. You are performing a great service. You are assisting in the transformation of the consciousness of all humanity and all souls in all universes.

Teaching by using direct soul communication has many benefits. I have already identified many benefits for those doing the teaching and for those receiving the teaching. The benefits do not end there. They extend to all humanity. There are numerous souls present at each teaching, souls who need to hear the particular teaching. These souls also benefit in the ways that have been identified. This is a wonderful blessing for these souls who are present only in soul form. They need to learn the lessons of the teaching in order to make progress on their soul journeys. They need the virtue connected with the teaching. Because teaching done in flow has a very high frequency and vibration, the benefit to these souls is great. They are able to enter into and receive wonderful light, which will empower them to continue on their journey. They receive great virtue by being present and listening to the teaching. In fact, teaching in flow is much more than teaching. It is also a blessing and a healing. This is a very important realization to keep in your awareness.

Every teaching can be a blessing and a healing. This is true in a special way when the teaching is done in direct flow. All of the teaching is coming from the Divine and from the Soul World. As the teacher, you are simply the one through whom the information, the blessings and the healings become present. You are a divine direct channel through whom all of this flows. The benefits for you, your listeners, the Soul World and all souls in all universes are significant. All of the teaching becomes part of your soul journey and also part of the soul journeys of all who listen. Over time, you and all who receive the teaching will gain deeper understanding as layers and layers of meaning continue to reveal themselves. When you first give the teaching, you have a certain level of understanding on the soul level. As you continue with the teachings or even in daily conversation, additional layers of wisdom connected with the teachings you have given will present themselves to you. You will hear yourself say things in daily conversation that will surprise you. You will have a new understanding about the topic that you presented. When people ask you questions about the topic, you will have insights that suddenly are present and available. All of this happens because your soul has received the message and is continuing to develop its understanding of the message. This is another wonderful benefit of teaching through direct soul communication. Moreover, all those who listen to the teaching benefit in the same way. The wisdom and knowledge they receive is like a seed. If they chant or do any other practice to stay connected to the teaching, they are watering the seed. It will grow. It will blossom. It will flourish. It will become the presence of beauty in their lives.

Teaching through direct soul communication is a very special gift. It is a profound service. It is quite possible for each of you to teach in this way. In Chapter 2, I described how to begin doing direct soul communication. Many of you will be able to follow the teachings and practices I have given to open your direct soul communication channel and begin doing direct flows. You can use this approach for any kind of teaching, not just teaching connected with Soul Mind Body Medicine. You can certainly use it for other teachings connected with the Soul World. You can also use direct flow to teach in ways that you may not realize are teaching. You may not be planning to make a formal presentation or give a public lecture, but perhaps you are going to be talking to a few friends about their ailments and some Soul Mind Body Medicine techniques for self-healing. This conversation will most definitely be teaching. You will be helping your friends gain some wisdom and understanding of Soul Mind Body Medicine, of their soul journeys, and of the essence of soul wisdom. This is teaching! Before and during your conversation, connect with the soul of Soul Mind Body Medicine. Ask for guidance on what to say next, on what would be most appropriate for your friends to hear. You can do this quite quickly.

Doing this kind of quick-checking communication will not affect the accuracy of your responses. Accuracy depends upon soul standing. It does not depend on how long you take to chant or prepare before you begin the soul communication. This is an important realization to keep in your awareness. Chanting definitely helps because it increases your soul standing. It helps to transform every aspect of who you are. Chanting definitely will assist you in improving you accuracy. If you are going to teach using direct flow, you should be sure your accuracy is at least eighty percent. Even greater accuracy would be wonderful, but eighty percent is very good. It is actually more accurate than many who call themselves professional psychics or readers.

To help you increase your soul communication accuracy and to uplift your soul standing, you can chant *Love, Peace and Harmony*. This Soul Song was given to me by the Divine on September 10, 2005 to bless every soul of humanity, Mother Earth and beyond. By chanting this Soul Song, you will be offering service. You will gain virtue. The more service you offer, the more your soul standing will increase.

Lu la lu la li

Lu la lu la la li

Lu la lu la li lu la

Lu la li lu la

Lu la li lu la

I love my heart and soul

I love all humanity

Join hearts and souls together

Love, peace and harmony

Love, peace and harmony

Chant this Soul Song every day upon waking up, before lunch or before going to sleep. It will help bring the qualities of love, peace and harmony into your life. At the same time, you are offering service to others. This is a great way to bless all aspects of your life and to increase the accuracy of your soul communication. I cannot stress enough that service through chanting is a key to improving your accuracy. Chanting *Love, Peace and Harmony* will develop your spiritual abilities.

When you teach in direct flow, you will also receive responses to questions from your audience. It is very important that you allow time for questions and answers. Hearing teaching in flow will be a new experience for many in your audience. As I have said, this kind of teaching is of a very high frequency and vibration. Consequently, your listeners may feel a bit shaky while you teach or afterward. This is quite normal. Do not be concerned. Let those who are listening know ahead of time some of the possible physical responses. Close your teaching with some grounding practices, such as those I mentioned in Chapter 2. If your listeners have none of these responses, then everyone has an opportunity to be very grateful.

Direct soul communication is a wonderful gift from the Divine and the entire Soul World to all humanity at this point in our history. It will be particularly valuable as we continue through this time of transition and purification for Mother Earth and beyond. We are honored and privileged to be able to participate in this transformation. We are honored and privileged to be able to assist all humanity, Mother Earth and beyond in their purification. We are honored and privileged to be able to flow divine teachings, to allow divine souls to "borrow our mouths." We are extremely blessed and totally grateful.

Third Eye

Third Eye images are also very useful for teaching. If your Third Eye is open, you may receive images while you are teaching. Some in your audience may have Third Eye images. Ask those in your audience what images they saw during the teaching. They could have much to share. Every image will add richness, depth, texture and insight to the words of the teaching.

Those whose Third Eye is not fully open will have fewer images or simply see light. All images received will be wonderful contributions to the teachings. The images will give greater clarity to many. For some, the images will offer another layer of teaching. Third Eye images of light are a very special kind of divine presence. The word "light" is quite inadequate, because people's Third Eye images of light have great variations in the quality, density and color of the light. Each of these variations has its own particular message. It is important for the receiver of an image of light to ask for the message associated with the image. If the message is given in the form of a direct response, that is excellent. If not, you could do a direct flow of the teaching connected with the quality and kind of light in the image.

Do not forget to remind everyone that Third Eye experiences will be different. Not everyone will receive the same images. Those who see light will have great variation in what they experience. However, there will also be consistency because the essence of the images will be the same. Sometimes people will say, "I only saw light." It is very important to help people understand that there is no "only" about it. Receiving images of light is a profound treasure. There is extraordinary wisdom and deep teachings connected with these images. However, people so easily get caught up in comparisons (avoid these, as

I have taught) and disappointment that they often forget to ask for the message of the image. Do not have the wrong impression that the image is the complete teaching. In most cases, we need to ask for the message to clarify the teaching. The image alone gives only a partial experience. The image itself is like one wheel of a bicycle. The message of the image is like the other wheel. With both wheels it is possible to move forward easily. It is possible to balance easily. If you only have one wheel, it is difficult to balance. It is difficult to move. Ask for the message. Add the second wheel and you can move forward in your soul journey more easily and in greater harmony.

In addition to images of light, people can, of course, receive images of the Divine, of the higher saints, of animals and other creatures from the Soul World, and of other places, such as Heaven's realm. The images that can be received are unlimited. For example, some people may see into their Message Centers as the teaching is taking place. These images can tell them about the transformation they are undergoing at every level of being.

The possible images are without limit because they come from the Divine and the Soul World, which are without limit. I cannot mention all the possibilities. I can only give examples. Some people with widely open Third Eyes can actually see a series of images, like a movie, that match the words of the teachings. For example, if the teaching is about the soul being in charge, they will see an image of the soul as a commander. If you as the teacher also receive images, that can be helpful. The images may guide you to points that need clarification or elaboration. If you do not receive images as you are teaching, that is also fine. You could avoid the distraction of seeing what you are saying. You may be able to stay in a much deeper connection with the Divine and the Soul World, and will better be able to stay in the condition of the teaching. Whichever happens for you is a blessing. Always say "thank you." Never complain because you do or do not receive images. Say "thank you" for whatever the Soul

World has given you. Their wisdom is infinite. What they give you is exactly right for you.

Those who do not receive Third Eye images will be most grateful when others share their images. When others describe their images, those who do not think they have Third Eye ability often begin to see what others are describing. They may realize that they saw what others saw, but didn't recognize it as a Third Eye image. Often, beginners do not recognize their Third Eye images because they expect an image with photographic clarity and detail. That will come as one's Third Eye abilities develop. However, beginners usually receive Third Eye images that are fuzzy, blurred, obscure and fleeting.

In addition to expanding and clarifying the teachings, Third Eye images can also be used to give teachings. You can use your Third Eye images in a way similar to direct flow. You can watch what the Third Eye images are doing and saying, and convey that as your teaching. This requires highly developed Third Eye abilities. Some people with advanced Third Eyes can not only see the images; they can also hear sounds and smell scents associated with the images. If they see a celebration, they also hear it. If they see a garden, they also receive the fragrance of the garden.

When you teach using Third Eye experiences, avoid getting bogged down in detail. Stay with the essence. This is very important. It is not desirable and often not possible to share all the details of your images. That would dilute the power of the teaching. Focus on the most powerful and most profound images. These are the ones that have the greatest impact on the soul journeys of others. Ask the most powerful images to give you the message that they want to share with all humanity at this time. The simple technique is, as always, to say *hello*. If you say *hello* to your Third Eye and the Soul World and ask them to show you only the most significant images, that is what they will do. Simply make the request: *Dear soul, mind and body of my Third Eye, I love you. Can you please share with me the most* *powerful images to see at this time?* This simple request will allow you to receive the most powerful images that will have the greatest impact on your audience. If you do not make this request, you may see everything from A to Z. Some of it may be very helpful, but some of it you may not be able to use at all.

Using images as your way of receiving teaching from the Soul World is a very powerful connection. The teachings and messages you receive are on a very high level. The frequency and vibration are on a very high level. The healing, blessing, rejuvenation and transformation that take place through these teachings are very powerful. Sometimes you will be able to describe things you see through your Third Eye that are heart-touching. Frequently, the most powerful Third Eye images are connected with past life experiences. If this is what you are teaching, it would be very helpful to share in a general way. However, do not identify a specific person. People, especially those who are starting on their soul journey in a conscious way, have the impression they are ready for anything, but that is not true. If someone wants to know about himself, he can make a private appointment with you, and you can then share the information in an appropriate way. Sharing information about an individual in a public setting is not appropriate. This kind of revelation can cause great harm. It can open soul memories that require a great deal of healing. It can open deep emotional wounds. It can slow the person's soul journey, creating bad karma for you. That is why personal information must be shared privately at the appropriate time, or not at all. Pay great attention to the seriousness of this teaching.

Third Eye experiences can trigger great curiosity and great interest. That is fine. What needs to happen is for that curiosity and interest to take the step to becoming a commitment to the soul journey. Some stay at the level of curiosity. That is a pity. Third Eye images have much more than "entertainment" value. There are so many possibilities. Staying at the level of detail wastes all of the wonderful possibilities for wisdom, healing, rejuvenation and transformation. This is quite unfortunate. If you have Third Eye abilities, keep these cautions in mind.

Offering your Third Eye experiences and using them to do teachings is a wonderful service. It is also great service to let those who are listening know that it is important to move beyond the focus on the details. Letting them know that it is absolutely necessary to connect with the message is itself a profound teaching. Third Eye images can also be a profound source of teaching for you in your own life. This is another aspect of teaching through Third Eye experiences that I will explain.

When you receive any Third Eye image, ask for its message, as I have explained. In addition, keep a record of the Third Eye images you receive. Speak to their souls. Ask the soul of each image what it is you need to learn. What new wisdom does it have to teach you? Are there practices it wants to show you? Third Eye images are particularly helpful when the Soul World wants to show you a new practice.

Those who have very active Third Eyes will not find it practical to keep a complete record of their Third Eye images. After all, you could be receiving images all day long. What you can do at the end of the day is ask your Third Eye to show you once again the most important images of the day for your soul journey. You might ask, for example, to see the three most important images. When you receive those images again, you have a new opportunity to ask for the message and the teaching of the images. Besides keeping a record of the three most important images of the day, you might also record the images that occurred most often throughout the day. If they occurred frequently throughout the day, they have something special to tell you. Receive their wisdom and teaching. The images that occur frequently throughout the day will often be playful ones that carry a message to be flexible, to keep a sense of humor and to have no attachment. Living this message makes it possible for you to experience authentic freedom and to enter into deep and authentic joy.

Receiving Third Eye images for yourself is a very special gift. You receive teachings, wisdom and healing tailor-made for you. All of this falls in the category of doing soul communication for teaching. If the teaching is directly to you, that is very useful. You will be able to use it to assist others. You will be able to teach others how Third Eye images have been guides in your spiritual journey and your healing journey. Whatever you receive for yourself, you will be able to use for others. As you develop your ability, more and more images will be given to you to help others. At the beginning of the development of your Third Eye, the images will primarily be to clarify a teaching or to assist you in your own soul journey. All of these images are wonderful treasures.

You can use any form of soul communication to connect with the message of a Third Eye image. You can ask directly and receive in direct flow. You can ask for more images. You can do Soul Language and translation. And sometimes you will have direct knowing that a particular teaching or wisdom is connected with a Third Eye image. All of these ways of receiving information are helpful but you will usually use only one of these ways to understand a particular image. For another Third Eye image, you could use a different way of connecting with the message.

Direct knowing is a particularly high-level ability. If you receive a message, you receive it through knowing. Once your ability reaches this level, you will only improve. Your frequency and vibration will increase. Your direct knowing will become highly accurate. You will begin to experience it as the way you approach everything in day-to-day life. This will be particularly true when you are connecting with the message of Third Eye images.

Third Eye images are very helpful to share with those who are beginning their spiritual journey, or with those who have not developed this ability. Being able to see what is happening in the Soul World is very helpful. It is not essential, but it can be very useful. It is like having your eyes open when you are watching a movie. You may still be able to understand the content of the movie with your eyes closed, but seeing the images makes a great deal of difference.

Those who have developed great ability in doing direct flow will often receive the same information; however, they will receive it through words. They will have a verbal picture. One way or another, the Soul World provides the information that is needed. It provides the teaching and the wisdom the way it is needed. It provides through the channel that is most helpful to the individual. The Soul World gives each person the most appropriate method to access the spiritual wisdom and teaching. If your method is through the Third Eye, good. If your Third Eye ability has not yet developed, that is also good. Whatever you have been given is your particular gift from the Divine and the Soul World. Use it well. Use it for teaching. Use it for service.

When you receive Third Eye images, you are opening to an aspect of the Soul World and the Divine that is very sacred. Being able to receive these messages is an honor and privilege. Being able to share what you have received with others is a great benefit and great service.

Soul Language and Translation

You can teach through Soul Language and translation. You can teach any topic using this method. You can translate your own Soul Language. You can ask someone else to translate. If you are teaching a class or workshop, it is best to have at least one other person present who has a highly developed ability to translate.

Let me use "service" as a sample topic. If you are teaching this topic, speak about it in Soul Language for one or two minutes and then have someone translate. A person who has developed a high level of translation ability would be ideal. Have three to five people offer a translation. Some in your audience may be puzzled that there can be five different translations of the same Soul Language. Let me explain how this happens.

Your Soul Language translation flows from your Message Center. If your soul standing is very high, the frequency and vibration of your translation will also be very high. If your soul standing is lower, the frequency and vibration of your translation will be lower. However, everyone who translates the Soul Language will connect with the essence of its message. Each person's translation will express it differently. Each person's translation will offer different details. The depth of the wisdom and teaching will differ across the various translations. But, *the essence will be the same.*[21]

Soul Language translation is a powerful tool. It is an extraordinary gift of increased virtue. You already know that Soul Language is a very pure form of communication. It is the means of communication used by your soul and by the entire Soul World. Therefore, translating Soul Language is a very special privilege and honor. Doing translation is obviously a special connection with the Soul Language. It is a special, very pure connection with the Soul World. This is why Soul Language translation should be approached with great reverence, honor and appreciation.

The greater your appreciation for translating Soul Language, the better you can go into the condition of the Soul Language and its message. When you go into the condition, you are better able to translate accurately. In fact, this is really the secret to translating accurately. Go into the "hero condition," which in this case is the condition of the translation.

When you teach through Soul Language and translation, keep your Soul Language brief. You can easily teach for an entire hour using short segments of Soul Language. For beginners, it is especially important to stick to short segments. Even for those who are more advanced in their abilities, short segments are desirable. The audience will be able to follow short segments much more easily. An additional benefit is that more people will have an opportunity to give translations when you keep your teachings brief. You do not need to worry about being able to complete your teaching. It will happen. All the ideas and the wisdom needed for your particular lecture or workshop will be given to you.

You could supplement and amplify the Soul Language translations with some teaching in direct flow or by summarizing and developing the essence of the teaching with more details and examples. You can develop each segment of the teaching if you wish. As the teacher, it is your responsibility to stay connected with the topic and with the Soul World, the Divine and the souls of all who are present. As you listen to the translation, you can comment on the essence and then develop the teaching. After you do that, begin the next segment in Soul Language. Continue this process.

Another way to teach using Soul Language and translation is to do simultaneous translation. You would speak the teaching in Soul Language in a very quiet tone of voice. At the same time, another person would translate in a louder tone of voice. Simultaneous translation is a very powerful and very effective way to do teachings. Of course, you need someone present who can do simultaneous translation with great accuracy. Simply ask the souls of those present, "Do you have the ability to do this?" If no one responds, then you know you cannot use this approach.

Using Soul Language and translation is a very important aspect of soul communication for teaching. Numerous benefits result for each person when Soul Language and translation are used. Many souls throughout the universe can enter into the essence of the teaching in a profound way. The possibilities of using Soul Language and translation for teaching are without limit. The possibilities are powerful, profound and beyond our imagination. There will be a time when people who speak different languages can attend the same lecture and receive all the benefits available because it will be done entirely in Soul Language. We have the privilege and opportunity to introduce this approach to teaching worldwide. We are very honored and very blessed.

Notes

[21] In some situations, someone's "translation" could carry a message or essence that is clearly different from other translations. This is a signal that the translation is not correct. This happens when there is an attempt to interpret using the logical mind. The use of the logical mind could be conscious or unconscious. Anxiety, lack of confidence and other emotional and mental factors, and even physical factors, can block one's ability to offer a true translation.

Soul Communication
as Service

Service is the purpose of life. Service connects us with the Divine, with the entire Soul World and with the universe. All soul communication abilities — Third Eye, Soul Language and translation, direct flow, direct knowing — can be used to offer service. In fact, every time you use soul communication, it is service. However, in this chapter I will discuss using soul communication consciously for the primary purpose of offering service. Every soul communication channel is a direct link to the Divine and the Soul World. Using those links to serve others is a profound honor and a wonderful privilege.

Receiving Messages for Others

One way to use soul communication for service is to receive messages for others. People who know you have soul communication abilities will often ask you for this service. This type of service could be a vocation. When you serve others in this way, you are able to link with the Divine, one of the highest saints, the person's own soul or the soul of someone who has transitioned and receive the message. You have the honor and privilege of being the voice for that message. It is your voice. The message and the teaching belong to the Divine, the highest saint or whatever soul has given the message. Always acknowledge that it is only your voice. The message has a different source. Always thank the source of the message.

Your accuracy will improve rapidly when you express this awareness and gratitude. Some of you may feel a bit shy or reluctant to make this acknowledgment. Shyness and reluctance are reminders that your ego is active. I cannot emphasize enough how important it is to acknowledge that it is only your voice and that the teaching and the message come from another source. You must also express gratitude to the source of the teaching. When you do this, you will be blessed in abundance, and the frequency and vibration of the messages you receive will increase.

If you are the person who is asking for information, the message you receive is sacred, profound and transforming. It must be treated with great reverence and respect. You must be willing to act upon the information received. To ask a question of the Soul World is to create a contract. If you are not going to keep your part of the agreement by acting upon the information you receive, then do not ask the question. This is very serious. If you are given information by the Divine or the Soul World, but then decide not to use it, you are saying that their information is not important. You are saying that you know better than the Divine. This is not a good choice. It can have harmful effects for you. It would be much better not to ask in the first place.

If you are the one doing the soul communication, it is very important that you keep your Message Center open. Stay continuously in the condition of being the voice for the source of the message. When you stay in the condition, the message that flows through you is accurate. It is a blessing and a healing. If you allow yourself to think about the message received, you are no longer in the condition. You are no longer the voice for the source of the message. Go back into the condition by reconnecting with the soul who is giving the message.

If the person who has asked you to connect with a particular soul has more than one question, it is a good idea to have the questions come from the flow that you receive. Answer the person's most important question first. You do not need to know the other questions. Frequently people who have many questions are surprised as they begin to hear the first response. Very often the first response will also include responses to other questions or concerns. So instead of having ten questions, they may discover they really only have two or three, because the responses to all the other questions have been included in the other answers. This type of flow is possible when you stay in the condition and when the person who is asking the questions has made the commitment to use the information that is received.

Sometimes people ask for guidance through soul communication out of curiosity. They don't know exactly what decision they need to make. They may be considering several possibilities and want some input on the best choice. Their intention is to take the information and then think about it. For them, it is a fact-finding activity. They will ultimately use logical thinking to come to a conclusion. If people come to you with this approach, you must explain to them that *they are expected to act upon whatever information they receive.* To receive a message from the Divine or a highest saint simply to satisfy one's curiosity is not a good idea. The suggestions given are from the highest sources. To discount the information and continue to use logical thinking to make a decision is a major spiritual discourtesy. I cannot emphasize enough how important it is to act upon the information given. I also need to remind the recipient that what you receive needs to fit practical concerns. If it does not, then it is not accurate. It is very important to keep this balance. I am not saying that you must accept every single word you are given. There is not a single soul communicator with one hundred percent accuracy. If you are the one doing the soul communication, remind the other person of this.

When I say that guidance must be in harmony with practical life, that does not mean the suggestions will always be comfortable. In fact, they will rarely be comfortable. We are always asked to do more. We are always asked to raise our soul standing. We are always asked to become more of an unconditional universal servant. We are always asked to offer a pure quality of total GOLD. There will always be a challenge in the response received. The person who has asked for the soul communication needs to be prepared for a challenge.

When you do this type of soul communication and teaching, you are offering a precious treasure to the other person. You are assisting in that person's soul journey at a profound and deep level. The questions you are asked may not explicitly connect with the soul journey. The questions may be about a relationship. They may be about a job. They may be about interactions in the workplace. The possibilities are without limit. But no matter what the questions are, the responses will always connect with the soul journey in some way.

For example, the questions might be about how to bring about physical healing. The response will absolutely be connected with methods for physical healing. However, to heal physical health issues, the soul must also receive healing. This is only an example to help you understand that every issue will connect with the soul journey in some way. Some of these connections will be very direct. Others will not be as direct. However, they are every bit as important. Do not be surprised if the response addresses the person's soul journey.

As I said, the response will sometimes be very challenging for the person. Often, the more clear and direct the response, the more challenging it will be. Some responses will give two or more possibilities, and the Divine or the highest saint will say to the person, "You must choose." This is a particularly powerful type of message. The soul that gives the message will make it very clear what the advantages and disadvantages of each option are. It will be very clear which option is the best for the soul journey. However, the Divine, the highest saint or whatever the source of the message will not force the person to act in a particular way. The person who receives the message must make that choice. The person will need to move more in the direction of commitment. To make the best choice is to make a significant commitment.

If no options are given, the person simply needs to act upon the guidance given. If choices are given, the person needs not only to receive the wisdom and the teachings, but also to release all blockages to commitment. Choices are given so that the person can freely choose for his soul journey. The best choice for the person's soul journey will also be the best for all the other souls involved. This last statement may not always be obvious. However, its truth will become clear in time.

It is a particular challenge to have options when you ask for direction. If this is your experience, you might want to ask a question about why the soul who is giving the response has given you so many choices. Why not just one clear response that you can follow? There is great wisdom to be gained in the answer to that question. The answer will be a little bit different from person to person, but basically the essence of each response will be as I have suggested above.

You offer great service to another when you do direct soul communication, or any form of soul communication. You have been the presence for the responder. You have given teachings, blessings and healings. All of this is profound service. It is transforming for you as well as for the other person. When you are offering this type of service, you are connecting with the entire Soul World and its wisdom. You are receiving what is needed by the person who has asked for

your help. You receive what can be used by that person. It is important to let the other person know that he must be ready to act upon
whatever he receives.

The messages that you receive for others have the possibility of
transforming their lives. If they have asked you a question of the
Divine, you have the honor and privilege of speaking that message
for the Divine. You have the possibility of helping the other person
hear what the Divine wants them to live at this moment. You will
be amazed at how very often the message from the Divine is one of
the most tender and gentle love. The struggle for most of humanity
at this time is to accept the reality of the Divine's love for each one.
Many individuals find it very difficult to enter into the experience
of the unconditional love of the Divine. This message is a treasure
to speak for another to hear. It is a treasure to make available to
all humanity, Mother Earth and beyond at this time. Knowing how
profoundly loved we are changes all of life. I have said many times,
"Love removes all obstacles. Love melts all blockages." When one
hears and receives the message of divine love, the most extraordinary transformation can occur. Receiving the message will be followed by acting upon it. The Divine's suggestions to make this love
become the very air that we breathe must be followed. The suggestions will be very simple, but they will be transforming. All of life
will be different.

When you give this message to others, it is important to say it in
ways that others can receive and accept. When the Divine expresses
love, it is done in a very strong yet gentle way. It is the message that
humanity needs at this time. Accepting and acting upon this message will bring about rapid transformation in every aspect of life.
What is amazing to me is that people can hear this message over and
over again in many different ways and still not "get it." The Divine
has sent messengers throughout the ages to manifest how important each one is to the Divine and how deeply loved each one is by

the Divine. Still, this message needs to be received and accepted by most of humanity.

When you do soul communication for others, do not be surprised if you receive messages of divine love over and over. This is the message the Divine has for humanity at this time. It is the message the Divine has given throughout the ages. It is the message that opens the door more fully to the Soul Light Era. Some who come to you will need to receive this message over and over again. Sometimes it will be stated in exactly the same way. Sometimes it will be stated differently. That does not matter. It is a message of divine love. Those who receive this message need to act upon it. That means they need to act in a way that demonstrates they are experiencing divine love. They need to manifest in their lives that they are loved. This will be evident in a variety of ways. One way is that they will find it easy to forgive. Their conversation will change. Complaints and criticism will be replaced by gratitude. They will experience transformation on every level in their lives. They will become the presence of divine love, which means they will carry divine joy. What wonderful gifts to bring to those who come to you for soul communication!

This direct soul communication will give others the tools — the information, teaching and wisdom — they need to enter more fully into their soul journeys. It will assist in healing their physical issues and emotional issues. It will assist in healing their egos and in releasing their mindsets, attitudes and beliefs. Most especially, it will connect them with the reality that they are held in divine love and that they have the honor and privilege of manifesting divine love to all humanity. Many of those who come for soul communication will already have an appreciation of this reality. All they need are teachings on how to *become* the presence of divine love to a greater degree in everyday life.

Doing soul communication to answer these questions is a very high level of service. You who receive these teachings and information will act upon what you hear. You will then share it with others — in words and through actions. Your service will spread and multiply through the others' service when they act upon the message. Also, countless souls throughout the Soul World and throughout the universe listen to every direct soul communication you do. Their transformation is also part of your service of doing the soul communication. It benefits the soul journey and the physical journey of the one who has come to you. It also benefits the countless souls who have been present for the teaching.

When the Divine teaches, every soul listens. When the highest saints teach, countless souls listen. When your guides or healing angels teach, countless souls listen. When the soul of Mother Earth teaches, countless souls listen. You are assisting not only the one to whom you are speaking directly; you are assisting countless souls. The service that you offer by doing direct soul communication for a single person extends far beyond that person. You have the honor and privilege of assisting all humanity and all souls to receive the messages of divine love, of the need for greater commitment, of how to heal physical issues, and so forth.

It is quite extraordinary to realize that you are offering service to all of these souls. It is a great blessing and a profound privilege to do soul communication that is service to so many. The more often you do soul communication and receive messages for others, the more frequently you can assist all souls to understand the teachings that have been requested by a single person. The issues experienced by one person are issues experienced by many souls. The struggles of one person are the struggles of countless souls throughout time and throughout the universe.

The transformation experienced by the one who comes to you will be experienced by countless souls. Service is offered for all humanity, Mother Earth and beyond. It brings about the transformation of the consciousness of humanity and all souls. It is a major contribution to the transition Mother Earth is experiencing. It helps in the purification process of Mother Earth and beyond. Receiving messages for others is a very special blessing and gift. If you do this as your profession, that is a wonderful blessing for you. If it is an occasional vocation, that is also a wonderful blessing.

Many of you will do soul communication for others as part of daily life. Co-workers might stop by with a simple question that can be answered in a couple of minutes. Every opportunity you have to receive messages for others is a precious gift. Use these opportunities to be the voice for the Divine, a high saint or another soul in the universe. Know that you are offering profound service for countless souls, not just the one who is asking you directly. You are blessed indeed.

Let us join hearts and souls together now to offer each other love. This blessing will help each of us become connected to God's heart and to all the higher saints and souls of the universe in a very intimate way. Love will melt all blockages. Our health can improve greatly. Our spiritual channels can open widely, vastly improving our ability to use soul communication. We will be serving all humanity when we offer love. Simply ask the Divine for a blessing: *Dear soul, mind and body of the Divine, I love you. Can you offer me a blessing of divine love? I am honored and appreciative. I cannot thank you enough. Thank you. Thank you. Thank you.* Then chant *divine love, divine love, divine love, divine love* for three to five minutes, the longer the better. As you receive the blessings of divine love from God's heart, you will in turn be able to love all souls more deeply and more unconditionally. You will be able to serve them much better. When you offer love, you have the ability to transform the lives of others. You have the ability to transform your own life. This is a key to improving your soul communication abilities.

Receiving Direct Communication for Yourself

In addition to receiving soul communication for others, you can certainly receive soul communication for yourself. I have described some aspects of this in previous chapters. How can you receive direct communication for yourself as service? You can receive messages that answer a particular question that will help your soul journey and the soul journey of others. If you are one of my students, you can receive messages about the divine mission. Even if you are not one of my students, the divine mission is an excellent topic for direct communication.

Simply ask, "What do I need to know to help bring about the transformation of the consciousness of humanity?" You can ask this question every day. There is no end to the information that can be received. It would be excellent to focus on this cornerstone of the divine mission.

To further ask, "What do I need to know to help bring about the transformation of the consciousness of all souls in the universe?" will take more practice. You will receive profound and helpful answers and teachings. However, I suggest you begin with asking about humanity. You will probably receive more useful and practical guidance. As I said in the previous section, when you receive the response, all souls will be paying attention because the response is given by the Divine. If it is a response from the highest saints, countless souls listen. So you serve all souls in the universe in a way that, although indirect, is very powerful.

To ask how you can assist in the transformation of the consciousness of humanity is a profound question. You could ask more specific and detailed questions, such as, "What do I need to know to bring about this transformation? What teachings do I need? What transformation do I myself need to assist in this transformation of the consciousness of all humanity? What healing do I need? Where do I need to improve? What is the most important aspect of my soul journey to transform? What do I need to release to better help bring about the transformation of the consciousness of humanity?"

Each one of these questions has infinite possibilities. The Divine will not run out of wisdom in responding to any of those questions. When you ask any question, you must have the same mindset that I described earlier. You must be willing to act upon the teaching received. If you are not willing to act upon the answer, do not ask the question. Ask a different question. You might even ask, "What question do I need to ask? Please make clear to me what I need to know and what I need to transform."

If you are just setting forth on your soul journey, good questions would include: "Please give me a teaching that I will be able to act upon. Please help me learn how to increase my commitment. How can I live in total GOLD? What does it mean to be unconditional?" All of these are excellent questions. All of them will assist you in transforming your consciousness. As your consciousness transforms, so does the consciousness of all humanity and all souls in the universe. Divine generosity allows for this continuous benefit. It helps you understand how profound it is to ask a question of the Divine or the highest saints.

We are honored and privileged to be able to do this. We can never say "thank you" enough. We can never give enough honor and respect for this privilege. Being able to communicate to receive direct messages is a treasure given to humanity at this time. This is a significant part of Mother Earth's transition. This is a very important period in the Soul Light Era. We are beginning to announce a new way of living, of being present, of being beings of light. That humanity now has available the possibility of direct communication with the Divine and highest saints is a vital part of this unfolding.

In previous eras there were a few select individuals who were able to do direct soul communication. This ability was not available to thousands of people at any one time. Most people did not even know such a thing was possible. We are living in an era in which all humanity will eventually be able to do direct communication, and it will be of a very high quality. At this time we are just at the threshold of developing this ability. The number of people who have developed this ability is still quite small, in the thousands at most. In this early stage of the Soul Light Era, that number is beginning to increase. When you do direct soul communication and ask the questions I suggested at the beginning of this section, you are assisting humanity to develop the ability to do soul communication. The more each one develops this ability, the more this ability is available to every other person on Earth. It is like a huge pool of light that humanity can dip into and drink from. This pool is the source of direct communication.

As each person does direct communication, this pool becomes bigger and bigger. Its quantity and its quality increase. As each person does soul communication, accuracy improves. Those who are already very accurate will become more accurate. Those who are not as accurate will improve. This takes place through individual practice. However, it also takes place because those who have developed the ability to do soul communication are using their ability. Simply using this ability is service to all humanity. Using this ability increases the quality and quantity of light that is available for all humanity to do soul communication. You offer service simply by doing soul communication.

In this Soul Light Era, soul communication will be essential. Direct soul communication is a unique blessing. We are the ones to bring this gift to all humanity. Never before have thousands, much less millions, had this opportunity. In history, this gift was given to only a few chosen souls. We are honored. We are blessed to receive this gift. Now, we must develop this ability. We have the honor and responsibility to bring this gift to others.

There are many ways to bring the gift of direct soul communication to others. First, and most important, is to develop your own ability. The more you use this, the deeper and more profound your connection to the Divine and the entire Soul World becomes. Each time you do divine soul communication, you connect with the hearts of the Divine and the highest saints. You connect with their message, which is their essence. There are no words to explain how special this is. Connecting with the message of the Divine transforms your life and your soul standing in the most profound way. At this time, there is no other way that is as powerful.

Connecting with the message of the Divine is possible because this message is very much needed. You have heard that the Divine is a universal servant. Allowing each person to connect with the divine message is the most complete service that can be offered at this time. You have the honor and privilege of giving words to the message. The message is exactly what is needed by humanity, Mother Earth and beyond. When you give words to the message, the Divine teaches in a direct way. Think about that for a moment. You express divine teachings for others. This is the highest service. You also express the message of the highest saints. Each one of the highest saints has a particular message for humanity, Mother Earth and beyond at this time. Each one has a particular teaching, wisdom, healing and set of abilities that are needed. They must become available now to assist in the transformation of the consciousness of humanity. The Divine is giving us direct soul communication to make all of this available.

At this time, Mother Earth is in a troubled condition. Humanity is suffering and struggling. Many feel lost and confused. The teachings that come through direct soul communication will help to heal all of these situations. They will bring humanity to a new level of consciousness. They will bring all souls in all universes to a new level of consciousness. When you do divine soul communication, you make all of this available. The Divine and the entire Soul World give teachings all the time. They serve us continually. The problem is that not everyone can hear the messages clearly. Not everyone can receive the images clearly. Some do not understand what they do receive. Many cannot hear or see at all. Those who do divine soul communication are given this blessing so that they can share it with others. This makes it possible for humanity to receive with clarity and simplicity the teachings, healings and blessings needed during this troubled time.

This is the beginning, but it is not enough. As humanity, Mother Earth and beyond go through the transition, the messages will need to continue. In fact, the need for divine soul communication will be even greater. As the transition accelerates, life will become very difficult for everyone. In their compassion, kindness and generosity, the Divine and the highest saints will not abandon us. The more difficult the struggle, the more powerful their teachings will be. Divine direct soul communication will serve many. It will help many through the transition. It will help initiate the next phase in the Soul Light Era.

As the transition moves to a new phase, and humanity, Mother Earth and beyond move to a new level of consciousness, there will continue to be a need for divine soul communication. When humanity reaches this phase of the Soul Light Era, soul communication will begin to blossom on Earth like a beautiful garden. Those who have brought the gift of divine soul communication will tend the garden. They will assist others to develop their abilities. They will assist others to serve. The quality and level of the teachings will change.

It is important to know what is waiting for us on the other side of Mother Earth's transition. It is important to know the role soul communication has to help accelerate this transition. Each one who does divine soul communication brings so much more than words to humanity and Mother Earth. Every word is a blessing. Every word transforms your soul standing. Every word is a healing. Every word rejuvenates. Every word brings the presence of the Divine to humanity, Mother Earth and beyond. All of this is also true for each of the highest saints. When you do divine soul communication, you are divine presence in a unique way. You are the presence of the highest saints in a privileged way. There are no words to express what an honor and privilege this is. There are no words to fully express how powerful this service is.

For hundreds, thousands and even more to practice divine soul communication and to be this divine presence brings a level of divine light and service that is needed at this time. It is the way the Divine wants to be present. It is the way the highest saints want to be present. When they are with us in human form, their presence is limited. When their teachings are expressed through soul communication, their presence is multiplied and potentially unlimited. Countless numbers of people will receive their teachings, healings, blessings and wisdom and learn their practices.

There is a special group of divine soul communicators whom I call Divine Writing Channels. Each receives a direct download of a specific topic. The topic is the one most suited to that Divine Writing Channel and most needed at this time. All that I have said about divine soul communication applies to the Divine Writing Channels in a profound way. The messages they receive become books. You know how many people can read a book. People share books with their friends and loved ones. Books are available in libraries and other public places. Every time a Divine Writing Channel's book is read, the Divine is present — teaching, blessing, healing and transforming.

The Divine Writing Channels offer a most powerful service. The books they bring into physical form are the teachings needed at this time. However, their messages have layers and layers of meaning. These books will become more and more important as the Soul Light Era continues. Remember, these teachings are from the Divine and the highest saints. Every time someone reads one of these divine books, he will move to a new level of understanding. He will have his soul standing uplifted. His soul communication channels will open more fully. Healing, rejuvenation and transformation will accelerate.

Reading these divine books puts you in divine presence in the way the Divine has chosen. The Divine becomes present to you in the way the Divine wants to be present. It is amazing to think that such a gift is being offered to humanity at this time. It is special to realize that ordinary human beings have the opportunity to be this kind of channel. It is easy to understand how transforming it is to be this kind of channel. Those who offer this service accelerate their soul journey in a way that is most profound. As they are flowing their books, they are literally in the presence of the Divine. They are divine presence. They are the presence of the highest saints. There are no words that can fully explain how profound this experience is.

Those who do divine soul communication not only serve humanity. This service is offered to all souls in all universes — the Light Side and the Dark Side. All souls receive the teachings and the blessings. They enter into transformation and are healed. Their consciousness moves to a different level. Divine soul communication is a tool. It is also a treasure. It is a treasure for the one who does the divine soul communication. It is a treasure for all those who receive it. It is a treasure for those who are Divine Writing Channels and for those who read the books they flow. This treasure only multiplies as it is used. The blessings become more abundant every time divine soul communication is done and every time a divine book is read.

I have said Mother Earth is in a troubled time. Many are aware how serious this is. We are blessed because the Divine has given us a way to soften these times. We have been given a way to heal these troubles. It is as if the Divine is giving humanity a map showing us the way through these troubled times. Divine soul communication gives us this map. It softens the intensity of Mother Earth's transition.

The Divine and the highest saints are with us in a special way. It is much more than being with us. Some people have the idea that the Divine and the highest saints are beside us or looking upon us. This is not correct. When you do divine soul communication, you *are* divine presence. This is what it means to say the Divine and the highest saints are with us in a special way. At this part of the Soul Light Era, those who do divine soul communication are paving the divine path for all who will follow.

This gives you only a small hint of what will follow. For now, it is enough to say that we cannot imagine the next phase of the Soul Light Era. It is enough to say that divine presence will become our environment. Those who do divine soul communication at this time are helping to create this new environment. Divine soul communication is assisting humanity, Mother Earth and beyond to transform their consciousness and their hearts.

It is such a pity that so many have turned their hearts from the Divine. Their hearts have become very small and, in some cases, very hard. Their hearts have been polluted by the world around us. All of this is in the process of changing. One of the most powerful agents of this change is divine soul communication. Those who use this powerful tool transform their hearts. They become connected to the Divine's heart and to the hearts of the highest saints. Divine soul communication makes this present to all humanity. The love, forgiveness, peace, healing, blessing, harmony, enlightenment and compassion that become present are beyond words. The more these qualities are present, the stronger their frequency and vibration.

I have said many times, "Love melts all blockages. Forgiveness brings peace." The frequencies and vibrations of divine presence will touch the hearts of many others. These frequencies, vibrations and light will radiate far beyond the ones who do the divine soul

communication. There is a possibility that many will begin to experience the expansion and softening of their hearts. Their priorities will
shift. They will move in the direction of service. They will leave the
pathway of selfishness, ego and greed. To be part of this process is
a profound blessing. Every time you do divine soul communication,
you are part of this process. This is what it means to bring about
transformation in the consciousness of humanity and all souls in
all universes.

You who do divine soul communication are part of a special
team. Many lifetimes have prepared you to be selected to participate
on this team. All of this preparation has given you the opportunity
to give greater service at this time. You have been chosen to be part
of a divine team. There are many levels of meaning to this term. To
be part of a divine team means that you work with the Divine. You
are the members, the Divine is the leader. Many of you have a favorite sports team. You know how much hard work and effort the
members of the team need to put in. You also know what an honor
and privilege it is to be on a special team. This is only a hint, a very
small picture of what it means to be on the divine team of soul communicators. You also assist one another just as members of any team
assist one another. The goal of this divine team is unique. It is the
transformation of the consciousness of humanity and all souls in all
universes. This is a divine team because the messages and the teachings are directly from the Divine. The blessings are directly from
the Divine. Everything that a team member does is connected to the
heart, soul, desire and commitment of the Divine. All that you do is
divine service. This is a privilege and an honor.

When you do direct soul communication you are offering divine
service. The benefits for you and others cannot be imagined. These
benefits are not limited to souls on Mother Earth. All universes are
included. All souls are included, in particular those in Jiu Tian. They
gather. They listen. They are also transformed and uplifted. When

this happens, they give you gratitude in the form of many flowers of virtue, and your soul's standing is significantly changed.

The teachings that are beginning to be revealed have been held in sacred trust for countless years. Many of these secrets will be revealed for the first time. Those who do direct soul communication will give voice to these ancient, sacred secrets. Those who are Divine Writing Channels will give form to these teachings. The topics for the Divine Writing Channels have been waiting to be revealed for many lifetimes. Some of these topics have been waiting since the beginning of history. The Divine Writing Channels will make this divine wisdom, knowledge and practice available to countless souls. They are offering tremendous service.

Doing direct soul communication also releases treasures that are waiting. Those who can do this need to take every opportunity they have to bring these teachings to humanity. Even if a particular topic is one that seems to be familiar and understood by many, I want to tell you that every topic is new. The teachings are new. The blessings, healing, rejuvenation and transformation that go with each teaching have never been present before in the way the divine soul communicators will make it present. Humanity is waiting. The highest saints are waiting. The Divine is waiting. We are very blessed.

I will give you a small example of teachings that seem to be familiar. This example is one connected with the Universal Law of Universal Service. People know how important forgiveness is. Many people have practices and belong to traditions that talk about forgiveness. This is a teaching that many traditions have presented to humanity for hundreds and thousands of years. The teachings available now through the divine direct soul communicators teach the transformation that comes from forgiveness. When forgiveness is viewed by itself, it is not complete. To have an appreciation of this divine quality, it must be seen to be connected with divine love. I have said, "When forgiveness looks in the mirror, it sees love. When love looks in the mirror, it sees forgiveness."

Many people find it easy to say, "I love you." For some, it is their common greeting. This is very good. But many who use this phrase only say the words. There is no heart connection. There is no connection to the heart of the Divine. And so the words become superficial. When these people hear that love and forgiveness are connected, they are challenged. Even those who say, "I love you" from their hearts and with a connection to the Divine can also be challenged by the intimate connection of love and forgiveness.

You cannot truly love until you also truly forgive. It is easy to tell when you have offered true forgiveness because you experience deep inner peace. This is your test. It is the way to know if your forgiveness is real. It is easy to fool yourself. It is easy to pretend. It is not easy to experience inner peace. This only comes from a real offering of forgiveness. It also comes from accepting forgiveness. Both of these actions are essential. Forgiveness is a gift given. It is a gift received. The inner peace that results is completely transforming. You literally feel it flow throughout your entire body. There is a shift. You will feel the tightness around your heart release. It can relax and be free. Your mind will automatically release some of its favorite mindsets, attitudes and beliefs. They will disappear like smoke in the wind. You will also feel very light. And you truly will be light. Your frequency and vibration will come so much closer to the Divine and the highest saints.

This is one small example of a teaching that is new for humanity. This teaching has been held to be released for the Soul Light Era. Humanity has always known that forgiveness is important. Humanity has not always known why or what the connection is with love and inner peace. Humanity has not had practical ways to give and receive divine forgiveness. In this era, there are many practical ways to do this. One way is to "go into the condition." While seated, put your left hand over your Message Center and your right hand in prayer position. Then, simply chant, "divine forgiveness." Continue to chant until you become divine forgiveness. Focus your attention on your heart, your Message Center and your soul. As you *become* divine forgiveness, invite the soul of the one you want to offer the gift of forgiveness. Tell this one to receive divine forgiveness. Tell this one he is forgiven. At this very moment, you are offering divine forgiveness because you are in the condition. The forgiveness is not coming from your mind or your emotions. It is coming from the Divine. The one you invited will be very grateful. Much of the karma connected with the situation will be cleansed. This is profound service.

In a similar way, *receive* forgiveness. Invite the soul of the one you have hurt, and ask this one for forgiveness. You might have to ask more than one time. You might have to offer blessings. However, remember to stay in the condition of divine forgiveness. This is very powerful. When you ask *in the condition,* your request is almost impossible to refuse. You can ask the other if there is anything you need to do to assist in his soul journey. When you have completed this offering and receiving of divine forgiveness, continue to chant and end by saying, "Hao. Hao. Hao. Thank you. Thank you. Thank you." You cannot thank the Divine enough for the treasure you have given and received.

This is a very practical tool for putting into practice the teaching on divine forgiveness. These practical tools have not been available to all humanity until this time. Those who do direct soul communication are honored and privileged to have the role, the task, the blessings and the gift of making all of this present for humanity, Mother Earth and beyond.

Communicating with All Souls in All Universes

In this book, I have shared many teachings on communicating with your own soul, with the souls of the highest saints and with the Divine. I have explained why this practice is important. You have also learned it is possible to communicate with the souls of your pets, your plants, a relationship, an emotion and countless other souls. You can ask for teachings from the sun, the moon, the stars, the solar system, the galaxy. You can do any form of soul communication with any soul in any universe. Communicating in this way will make a great difference in your soul journey.

When you do this type of soul communication, you will be amazed at the wisdom and soul secrets you receive. If you know the names of particular stars and planets, speak to them directly. Each one has its own unique soul, its own soul journey, wisdom, healing abilities and practices. You can gain much wisdom by doing this kind of soul communication. You can learn valuable lessons for your own soul journey. You can also learn valuable lessons about the long history of Mother Earth, our solar system and our galaxy. You can get a deeper understanding of why things are unfolding the way they are on Mother Earth. You can learn how Mother Earth's story fits in with the bigger story. You can learn on the soul level how very ancient she is.

The information you will gain from the Soul World is very different from the information scientists can measure with instruments. This does not mean that soul wisdom and science negate each other. It simply means there is much wisdom and knowledge that science cannot perceive, much less measure, at least not at the present time. We do not argue with science. We are not in conflict. We are on the same team and we are on the same journey. It is just that the information you receive from the Soul World very often will be different from scientific knowledge. "Different" does not mean "wrong" or "inaccurate." It simply means it complements and balances the information received from science.

There are many universes beyond this one. Soul communication allows you to communicate with all of these universes. They will tell you their stories. They will teach you their wisdom. Each one has a different story and a different quality to emphasize. Each one has a unique approach to healing practices. You can connect with and benefit from all of these teachings. Most people have not thought of doing soul communication in such an expanded way, but limit their communication to their "home" star or "home" planet.

Exploring all the possibilities of soul communication will bring great treasures to your life. Each universe and each galaxy has its holy beings and higher saints. You can learn great wisdom from them. It is not necessary to know their names. You can simply and directly address the highest saint in charge of healing. This form of address is quite appropriate and will do the job. After you address the highest saint, make your request as I have taught in previous chapters.

You can receive many delightful surprises from this form of communication. You may even discover that your true home planet is not Mother Earth. You may have lived and served on another planet, another star or a different universe for many lifetimes. You will learn the qualities and characteristics of this home place. This will give you great insight as to your own temperament and personality. It will help explain why for some there is always a sense of yearning to return home. Wouldn't this make a lot of sense if your home planet is not Mother Earth?

It is possible to receive teachings from every aspect of all universes. Just as Mother Earth has plants, animals, mountains and so forth, the same is true throughout the universes. The plants and animals most definitely are different. There are herbs in other universes. Some of them are very powerful. Learning the secrets of the herbs, plants and animals in other universes will help us greatly on Mother Earth. It is not necessary to have these herbs, plants or animals physically present with us. We can benefit greatly from a soul-to-soul connection. Ask the souls of these herbs and plants to offer healing to our health issues, emotional imbalances, mental issues and relationships here on Mother Earth. This would be of great benefit.

Let me teach you how to communicate with the soul of herbs to offer yourself a healing blessing for any aspect of your life. For example, if you have lower back pain, you can say: *Dear soul, mind and body of all the soul herbs in Heaven's herb garden, I love you. Can you please offer me a healing blessing for my lower back pain? I am honored and blessed. I cannot thank you enough. Thank you. Thank you. Thank you.*

Then, chant *divine herbs, divine herbs, divine herbs, divine herbs* for three to five minutes, or until you experience relief. Practice this daily if you have chronic pain. This is a simple and practical treasure that you can apply for self-healing.

Souls in all universes are happy to engage in soul communication with us. They are universal servants. They are eager and delighted to give service. When you do soul communication with them as I have described, you are giving them an opportunity to offer service, and you yourself are offering great service. Making this connection with other universes in order to learn from them is great service. One of the benefits is that the quality of light is different in various planets, stars, galaxies and universes. When you do soul communication with them, that quality of light becomes present on Mother Earth and contributes to her transformation.

The service you offer by doing this kind of soul communication has many aspects. You gain new wisdom. You learn healing practices. Your abilities increase. Your soul standing increases. You have made it possible for others to offer service to Mother Earth. You have brought a different frequency, vibration and quality of light to Mother Earth. You have made a direct connection with the virtue of various elements in all the universes. All of this is great service. Your soul standing will be uplifted. Your soul journey will be greatly transformed.

Along with the many benefits of communicating with all souls in all universes, it is necessary to keep in your awareness one caution. It is very important that you keep your body and soul present on Earth during your soul communication. During this lifetime, Earth is your home. The reason for that is that you have a particular and unique service to offer Mother Earth at this time and during the entire Soul Light Era. Since it is important that you offer your service on Mother Earth, it is absolutely necessary that you consciously keep your soul connected with your physical presence when you do this type of soul communication. It can be very harmful to you to allow your soul to go traveling all over the universes. To do this, you must have a very high soul standing. Very few people on Mother Earth have a sufficiently high soul standing to go traveling throughout the universes. Anyhow, this type of soul travel is not necessary. You can gain extraordinary information on a soul-to-soul level without ever leaving your physical body. Remote healing is powerful and, in some cases, even more powerful than face-to-face healing. Similarly, remote soul-to-soul communication is very powerful and effective.

Keep this caution in your awareness and follow this teaching. I am very serious when I say to you that you can harm yourself by allowing your soul to travel through the universes when you do not have enough virtue. It will be a huge challenge for some of you to accept this teaching. You may think, "Oh, Master Sha has taught about soul communication. Let me check to see if this type of soul travel is all right for me." Yes, it is true, I have taught about soul communication. I have also taught about false messages. I cannot emphasize enough how important it is that you follow my teaching on this point. Keep your soul and body connected in a conscious way.

Observe this caution and, when you do soul communication with all universes, you will be delightfully surprised at how grounded you feel. You will be amazed at how strong your Lower Dan Tian and Snow Mountain Area become. You will be delighted to discover how much further your spiritual channels open. All of this is possible for you when you follow the very simple teachings I have given in this section. I have mentioned only a few possibilities for soul communication with all universes. However, these examples will give you an idea of what is possible. You will think of many other ways that you can communicate with all souls in all universes. Enjoy the experience. You are very blessed.

Soul Communication in the Soul Light Era

The Soul Light Era is unique in the history of Mother Earth. Mother Earth has had many eras or "turns" in her millions of years of existence. These eras last 15,000 years each. We have just experienced the conclusion of the last 15,000-year era. The Soul Light Era, which began on August 8, 2003, is a new 15,000-year era. It is a unique "turn." It is the first time that the soul has been in charge to such a great degree. There have been other eras when the soul was most important, but the power of the soul was not as great as it is during this era.

Over the thousands and thousands of years of human existence, countless people have added their virtue. The highest saints have been guiding and blessing, healing and teaching over the years. We are honored to live in a time when the power of soul is so strong. In the Soul Light Era, we can truly say the soul is in charge. The soul is now much more powerful and influential in making decisions than it was in the previous era, which was dominated by the mind and the ego. The soul is now more powerful in influencing the choices that humanity makes. The soul is much more powerful in letting the mind know what it must do. The soul is very respectful, but it is also very conscious that this new era is one that will bring about unimaginable changes.

When more and more people are guided by their souls, many old patterns and behaviors will change. Institutions and societies will change. These changes will occur first on the level of the soul. They are reminders of what makes this era unique. It is important to keep in your awareness that many things we are experiencing now have never happened before. We are creating history in a new and different way. We are actually participating in bringing about a new creation. Everything that exists is in the process of changing. Everything that is familiar is changing. Some things that are familiar will, in many cases, continue on, but in a new way. Some qualities are recognizable. Other qualities are completely new to us. Even if we recognize situations, events and responses, we will also be aware that all of them are being experienced differently.

For example, there will always be teachers. When you hear the term "teacher," many of you will automatically think of your school days. This role of the teacher is familiar. When we use the term "teacher" in the future, it will be completely different. Schools will educate children in a totally different way. The emphasis will be completely different. Schools will teach a new consciousness. This consciousness will not be aligned with any religion.

Many other changes will occur. The role of the teacher will be one that is primarily concerned with connecting with the soul. Besides the changes in consciousness and changes in teachers themselves, the entire approach to teaching will change. In schools today – even those that are most creative and flexible – there are certain styles of teaching. They draw on experience. They build the strengths of the students, correct their weaknesses and focus on developing their minds. In the future, teachers will connect with the soul of their subject matter and the souls of their students, and teaching will be done soul to soul. This is an example to give you an idea of the changes that will come. This gives you an idea of what the Soul Light Era will be. Soul communication will have a special role in bringing all of this about.

Connecting the Past, Present and Future

With soul communication we have a much greater ability to connect the past, present and future. People try in many different ways to connect with the past in order to understand the present and shape the future. Soul communication is an excellent way to do all of these things. In fact, it will be very important to do this in the Soul Light Era. In this section, I will offer a simple teaching on how to link all three together: past, present and future.

Because we are at the very beginning stages of the Soul Light Era, we are still strongly influenced by the past. We have not experienced the fullness of Mother Earth's and humanity's purification. In some ways, we have one foot in the past and one in the present. We need very much to have both feet in the present. Soul communication helps us do this. In this section, I will focus on direct soul communication, which I also call direct flow. Understand that everything that I say about direct flow is also true for Soul Language and translation, Third Eye experiences and direct knowing. If it is more comfortable and familiar for you, you may think of Third Eye experiences or Soul Language and translation when I am speaking of direct flow. That is quite all right. Do not square your head. It is always important to be flexible. In a given situation, a certain form of soul communication will be best. In a different situation, another form will be best. When you are going to communicate with the past, take a few moments to connect with your soul communication channels and determine the channel through which the past prefers to communicate with you. This is showing respect and spiritual courtesy to the soul of the past and to the souls of your channels. I am only using direct flow as my "standard" example in this section.

Direct soul communication gives you very clear, concise and condensed information about the past. This can be information about your own past, the past of the country where you live, the area where you live, the organizations you belong to, the place where you work, the land where your home has been built, and so on. The possibilities are endless. Direct soul communication to receive information from the past is a very precious tool. Note that I used the word "from" and not "about." This is a very important distinction. To receive information *from* the past, you communicate with the soul of that past situation, organization or place. If you ask for information about the past, you are not necessarily directly connected with the soul of the past situation, organization or place. Communicating *with* the soul of the past brings a different kind and quality of information. It brings different teaching and healing. It touches a different part of your soul journey.

When you do soul communication to receive information from the past, you are allowing the past to tell its story. You are allowing the soul of the past to give its most treasured teachings. You are asking for its healing. You are allowing it to teach you its most important practices. All of these are powerful and precious treasures. To receive teachings and other gifts from the past helps give shape to the present. It gives you the setting and context for the present. When you hear directly from the soul of the past, you get a much clearer understanding of the present. You will appreciate what is most important for the present.

When soul communication is done with the past, respect is sometimes forgotten. There is such eagerness to learn what happened, who did it and why, that curiosity can become the focus. In doing communication with the past, these questions are important but they are not complete. I will teach you about other important questions. Always remember to say "thank you." The soul of the past is assisting you in ways that are truly amazing and most generous. The Akashic Records are assisting. They are giving you access to that part of the past you are asking about. Show respect to those in charge of the Akashic Records.[22] Show respect for all the workers on the Akashic Records.

When you do soul communication with the past, or any soul communication, it is important to acknowledge your mind's contribution. You also need to remind the soul of your mind that it is now time to allow itself to go off duty. This does not mean that you are suddenly going to become mindless or confused. When you allow the soul of your mind to rest, you become much more conscious, more able to think in alignment with your heart and soul, more able to experience clarity. But you do not need your mind to be active while you are doing soul communication.

Let me continue with the teachings about communicating on a soul level with the past, present and future. When you receive information from the soul of the past, you need to do something with it. As I said before, when you ask, you are responsible for acting upon the information you receive. If you do not want to act upon it, do not ask. How will you act upon information from the soul of the past? Use the information to give you a teaching about the present. Ask the soul of the past to teach you how this information has affected your present life. Many people have an awareness about their past, but they stay there. Their response regarding current behaviors, attitudes and beliefs is, "This is my karma." Or, "This happened in a previous lifetime and it has shaped this lifetime. In previous lifetimes I was treated badly and so, in this lifetime, I do not have confidence." Or, "In previous lifetimes I treated others badly and so, in this lifetime, I must suffer." There are many people who respond to information from the past in this way. This is not complete. You will not make much progress in your soul journey if you continue in this way.

Let me focus on one of these examples: "In the past I was treated badly and so, in this lifetime, I lack confidence." That is only the beginning of the story. Lack of confidence is connected with karma. It is also connected with many other things. You need to know all of that can and must be changed in your present lifetime. The information you receive from the past is only useful if you receive it as guidance for the things you need to change. If you know that you were treated badly in the past, then it is quite clear that there is a need for healing in the present. This healing must include forgiveness.

The past tells us how to approach the present. It tells us what the old patterns have been and it actually gives us the tools for changing them. People often use their past as an excuse: "This is the way I am" or "I have always been this way" or "In many lifetimes I have been this way." That is true. But it is not enough. These statements must be completed with, "Healing is needed. Love and forgiveness are needed. That is who I was. That is not who I am." Also, remember that we are in the Soul Light Era. The soul is in charge. In the past, the mind was in charge. Now, speak to the soul of your mind and tell it, "The experiences of the past are over. You no longer live there. This is a new era. This is a new chapter in your life. Perhaps it is even a new book."

Everything about the present is new. Your soul is helping you in every way possible to make the necessary changes. The entire Soul World is helping. Soul communication is a tool that will accelerate and bring clarity to the process. Using soul communication to learn how the past gives direction to the present is a very fast way to know what needs to be changed. It is a fast way to give healing to what needs to be changed. Soul communication will allow you to connect with the souls of unconditional love and unconditional forgiveness. You can connect with their souls nonstop, so that they can be your constant companions. They are the first two qualities in the universal law of universal service. They love to serve you.

So, when you look at the past, there is very little value in just looking. Use the past as a springboard to help you enter more fully into the present. Receiving information from the past frees you to live in the present. It identifies the mindsets, attitudes and beliefs that must be released. This is just as true for an organization, a society, a business or the ground upon which your home is built as it is for an individual. The same principles apply. Think of the past as the ingredients that you need to make the present. In some situations, the more ingredients you have, the more delightful the results will be for the present. However, there are some situations where very few ingredients are needed to make an absolutely wonderful dish. There is no need to continually go back to consult the past again and again and again. Receive the information you need, put it together and create the present. And know that all the ingredients are being combined in exactly the right way because you will do it by following the directions of the soul.

It sounds simple: receive the past as a set of ingredients to create the present. It is simple, but that does not mean that it is always easy. It can be easy if you remember to be guided by the soul and if you remember to always do soul communication. This will make the process faster and full of light. It will be an experience of gratitude.

Very often people hear these teachings and say, "Oh, this is so wonderful. Of course, I will do this." And then when they begin their next activity, all of the teaching leaves their awareness. They go right back to approaching everything through their minds and logical thinking. They stay stuck. To avoid this trap, make a practice of saying to yourself: *The past gives me the ingredients for the present.* This very simple statement can be used as a mantra. Saying it over and over again will literally change your mindsets, attitudes and beliefs. When you connect with the soul of your past, the past of Mother Earth, your organization or your business with the idea of receiving ingredients for the present, the response will be amazing. Great flexibility and creativity will be released.

I cannot emphasize enough that we are not limited or held bound by the past. The past opens the door for the present. It is a treasure chest but the treasures are to be used in and for the present. Even if your past includes many painful lifetimes, it is still a treasure. Each of those lifetimes gives you a priceless ingredient to help you create your present. This realization will give you a completely new response to your present situation.

I have used the term "free." It is important to realize that the kind of freedom I am speaking about is completely connected to respect and gratitude. It is the kind of freedom that allows you to be grateful for all that has been, and to respect it and receive it as a gift. When you have this response, the past transforms from being a burden to being light. Instead of bringing heaviness to your present, the past brings lightness. This lightness is freedom. This is what I mean by being free.

To change your response to the past by receiving it as treasured ingredients will in turn transform your response to all who are in your present. Everyone in your present has also been in your past. Some of these people can be challenging. Think of them as a rare and priceless ingredient. Cooks have some ingredients that are very precious and need only be used in small amounts. People who are challenging to you can be like these precious ingredients. Whether they are in your lives in small amounts or as constant companions does not matter. These challenging ones are the most precious ingredients because they help us create the present. They give us the most precious information we need. And they are vigorous in reminding us that there is a need for you to create something new. Say "thank you" to these challenges. Say "thank you" to all of your challenges. There is no substitute for these most precious ingredients given to you.

Let me use the example of making a cake. Many cakes need an ingredient such as baking powder to make them rise. Without baking powder, the cake will be flat. Think of the challenging people or circumstances in your present life. Know that they have a connection with your past. Think of them as the baking powder. They are the agent to bring about everything that needs to happen so that the cake will be excellent. In other words, challenging people and experiences are essential to help you bring about the changes you need to create a new present. Without them, the present will be flat and tasteless. With them, the present will become a new and wonderful treat. When you have this mindset, attitude and belief, your quality of soul communication will change dramatically. The level of teachings you receive will change. The way you live your life will change. The possibility of becoming the manifestation of gratitude will grow.

Doing soul communication will facilitate and accelerate your ability to look at challenges in this way. As a matter of fact, that can be a question you ask: "Dear soul of my past or of this organization's past, please identify the most challenging people, events and situations for me." Most people already know who and what is most challenging to them. However, there may be surprises. We usually think that our failures are challenges. However, it is also true that success is a challenge. Success can be the greatest challenge. When we are successful and surrounded only by people who are agreeable, there is very little room for transformation and service. And so, you might be surprised when you find out what is most challenging for you.

Once you have this information, next ask for a teaching on how this challenge can become a most precious ingredient. How will you practice using this challenge in daily life? When you use the teaching you receive, you will be amazed at how quickly you can release old mindsets, attitudes and beliefs. You will be delighted at how quickly you can create a new present. Your soul journey will accelerate. Your soul standing will increase. There will be changes in every aspect of your life.

Soul communication will facilitate all the possibilities I have presented. The only blockage is your mind. Soul communication can help you remove this blockage. I have already described some practical ways of using soul communication to remove mind blockages. Your soul wants to be totally involved in creating a new present for you. Your soul knows that this is its task. Your soul knows that this is what must happen in the Soul Light Era. Your soul knows you are one of the pioneers in bringing this approach to the Soul Light Era. All you need to do is decide and commit to do this. Let this be your daily mantra: *The past gives me the ingredients to create the present.* You can say this while you are commuting, shopping, walking, at work or in the shower. You can say this as you prepare to go to bed and when you get up in the morning. It is appropriate to use this mantra at any time of the day. You can also choose to set aside three to five minutes and simply chant repeatedly: *The past gives me the ingredients to create the present.*

It is very clear how interconnected the past and present are. Now, let us turn to the future. You can shape your future. I have offered teachings about creating a new present. A new present will also create a new future. When you become free of your past karma, when you release your mindsets, attitudes and beliefs, when you receive the past as the ingredients for the present, you have already changed the future. Any one of those actions changes your future. All of those actions together change your future profoundly.

When you have a completely new and different response to your present and live connected to the Soul Light Era, your future will also live connected to the Soul Light Era. The future follows the present. As your present becomes a new creation, your future becomes a new creation. This is a precious treasure that you can give to the future. You can pass this along to your children. You can pass it along to Mother Earth. All of your descendants will be blessed because you have made the choice to create a new present. You have made the choice to look at the past not as a burden but as a gift. The future will be very different. Your future and the futures of your descendants will be filled with light. Health, happiness, good relationships, success and long life will be part of those futures.

Soul communication is a tool to help you understand how the past becomes part of the present and how the present influences the future. When your present is shaped by the use of soul communication, you have access to profound wisdom, teaching and practices. You have access to sacred secrets that are now being revealed. Soul communication is a very powerful form of service. The more service you offer, the greater your virtue is. When I say that the present influences the future, these ideas are important to have in your awareness. Your future and the future of your descendants are affected by what you do now. Using soul communication connects you in a most profound way with the Divine and the highest saints. By doing soul communication, you are gaining virtue. You are bringing light to your soul journey. You are increasing your soul standing. You are accumulating many flowers. Your book in the Akashic Records becomes filled with light. These are wonderful gifts that you bring to your future and the futures of your descendants.

You know the familiar phrase about money and material possessions: "You cannot take it with you." When you leave this Earth, the only thing you take with you is your virtue. Virtue is spiritual currency. It is much more valuable than physical currency. Its value stays with you forever. Accumulating as much virtue as possible is the most generous thing you can do for yourself and your descendants. This is a practice of great wisdom.

To be able to influence your future is a wonderful gift. Most people do not understand the full significance of this very simple statement. Almost anyone you speak to on a spiritual journey would say, "Yes, I know I can influence my future." People do not realize how great that influence can be. Soul communication allows you to find out exactly how you can influence your future. It can tell you exactly what areas need to be influenced, and what you can do now to bring more benefits to your future. You can use any of the forms of soul communication. For example, your Third Eye can show you images of your future. You can then ask the soul of a future event what you can do in the present lifetime to change that event. For example, if you see illness, ask the soul of the illness what you can do now to transform the present so that this particular illness will not be part of your future. You can do this with Soul Language and translation or with direct soul communication. It is not selfish to do this type of soul communication. When you receive a teaching about what you need to transform in the present, many other people will benefit from your effort. Obviously, you benefit; however, each person you meet also benefits. When you transform any aspect of your being, you have more light to bring to each person you meet. This itself is great service.

When you learn those aspects that need transformation, when you learn what needs to be released, all those with whom you interact will benefit. Each one's mindsets, attitudes and beliefs affect one's own life journey. They also affect other people's life journeys. You may be the challenging one for another person. You may have an attachment to a certain belief, causing you to miss profound wisdom. You cannot share what you have not received. The more beliefs you release, the more wisdom you can access. You can manifest this wisdom to others in many ways. You can teach this wisdom in many ways.

Soul communication assists you to find out what it is in your future that your present needs to heal. It is wonderful to realize the possibility of having a future with excellent health, long life, loving relationships and successful business endeavors. These things are not only possible; they are realities. You connect with these realities through soul communication. For example, ask the soul of successful relationships what in your present life needs to change so that your future relationships will be positive and successful. You will receive very clear teachings and profound wisdom. You will also receive the healing blessings to make it possible for you to release what needs to be released in the present.

Soul communication gives much more than simple information. It is a soul-to-soul connection. This type of connection is profound. You can ask various situations in your future to guide you. Just as the past holds ingredients for the present, the future also holds ingredients for the present. The events, situations and life circumstances you desire are ingredients for the present. Ask for their wisdom and their teachings. Ask for their healings and blessings. With their guidance through the soul-to-soul connection, you can make different choices for your present.

I will emphasize again that if you ask the question, you must be prepared to use the answer. If you do not want to act on the answer, do not ask the question. When you receive a response, begin to use it immediately. There is always at least one aspect of every response that can be used immediately. If nothing else, you can say "thank you" for the opportunities you have been given. They are beyond words.

Using soul communication to influence the future and transform the present is similar to receiving a daily practice from the Divine. How many people would love to have a daily practice from the Divine and the highest saints? Many people spend a lot of money trying to find out how to do this. It is so simple. You only need to ask. If you want to know how you can influence your future so that it will be filled with light, health, longevity and success, just ask. Many people have personal trainers for their physical well-being. Using soul communication is the same as having a top-level personal trainer for your soul journey. This is a priceless treasure. You can never say "thank you" enough for this incredible opportunity.

The Divine is happy to serve. The highest saints are happy to serve. The souls of various events and circumstances in your future are happy to serve. They will tell you what you need. They will give you the practices you need. They will give you the teachings you need. If you need more specific details, all you need to do is ask. Some people ask for things as specific as information for their schedule for the day. Let me remind you again, you must use the information you receive.

Soul communication gives you the teachings that are specific for your life. They are specific for you at the time in your soul journey at which you are asking. When there has been healing for one aspect of your present, continue to ask, "What are the things in my future that can improve?" It is always possible to improve. Even if your future is free of illness, your health can still improve, so ask how you can do that. The response will give you information to help you further purify your present. The more pure you become, the more light you will bring to your future and the more your future will be shaped and blessed by divine presence.

Soul communication can do this for you as an individual. It can also do this for groups, for organizations and even for the land your home sits on. Because soul communication is connected with the Divine and the highest saints, there are countless possibilities.

I have shown you how to ask your future what it is in your present that needs to change. Another approach is to ask your present what needs to be healed and transformed so that your future will be one of light. The questions are basically the same. You will have an awareness of those things in your present life that are blockages. Speak to the souls of those blockages. You will receive the teachings to help you accelerate the removal of the blockages. If you are not certain exactly what the blockage is, you can ask: "Dear soul of this blockage, please tell me what you are. Identify yourself. Teach me how I can assist you to be transformed to light." It is very important that you invite the blockage to be transformed. You do not want to be rude and tell it to go away. You want it to become a better servant. You also want to serve it. You want to offer it unconditional love.

This may be a new idea for some. It is extremely important to practice this idea. Always offer love, whatever the blockage is. It may appear in your life as mindsets, attitudes or beliefs. It may appear as physical illness, difficult relationships or lack of business success. However it appears, offer unconditional love and invite it to transform. Imagine how grateful the soul of the blockage will be when it is treated with love and respect. It will want to serve you. It will be delighted to assist in your soul journey. It will also be happy that you are helping it to move to a higher level and be more filled with light.

This is great service. When you respond to the blockage in this way, you gain virtue on many levels. You gain virtue because you are offering service. You also gain virtue because of the gratitude being given to you. This gratitude comes to you in the form of flowers. The more gratitude you receive, the more flowers you receive. This is a most perfect win-win situation. It is a multiple win-win situation because countless souls are involved. Not only is your present involved, so is your future.

Another aspect of using soul communication as a connection between the past, present and future is the realization that the present is a bridge. The events of your past come into your present and, unless they are transformed, continue to the future. All the events from your past that also involved others are part of your present. Perhaps you have not encountered all of the events from your past in your current lifetime, but through your many lifetimes you most definitely will.

When you heal the past, you heal much more than just part of your own journey. All those who have been part of your past are also part of the healing process. When you heal a particular event, part of the healing will involve forgiveness. Forgiveness will bring freedom and virtue to all those who participate in it. When you do this for your past, you are doing it for others too, and this comes into your present. You will no longer need to learn lessons connected with those events. Instead of lessons, there will be light. And those from your past who received blessings will also experience light in their present lifetime. This is another form of service that is very profound and very powerful.

All that happens in the present influences the future. When transformation takes place, what continues on to the future is light. What a wonderful privilege and opportunity we have to serve so many souls and to bring our own soul standing to a higher level.

In this Soul Light Era, thousands and millions of people will learn how to do this kind of soul communication. We are only beginning the process at the first stages of the Soul Light Era. We are the pioneers, so it is our duty and responsibility to learn how to do these things well. We must use all of these teachings continually. We are transforming the past, present and future. We are creating the energy field that will allow others to learn rapidly. We are actually creating a field of light, and it expands far beyond Mother Earth. It is a profound honor and privilege to do this for humanity, Mother Earth and beyond.

Soul Communication and Mother Earth

Soul communication with Mother Earth has countless possibilities. Mother Earth has great wisdom. She is eager to share her wisdom. She has experienced much during her millions of years of existence. She is a very wise elder. When you do soul communication with Mother Earth, ask her for wisdom teachings. Treat her with the respect you would show an elder. You will be amazed at the depth of teachings you will receive.

You can ask for teachings on a particular topic. You can simply ask Mother Earth to share her wisdom with you. The more often you do this, the deeper and deeper the layers of wisdom will be. You might want to do this using Soul Language. Speaking the Soul Language of Mother Earth is a wisdom teaching just by itself. Translating her Soul Language will also be a wisdom teaching. Mother Earth also has her own soul song. It is different when you speak in general terms to the soul of Mother Earth and ask for a teaching. That will be one sound. When you ask the mountains for their wisdom, those will be other sounds. The teachings will be from the soul of the mountains of Mother Earth. You can ask for teachings from the rivers, the oceans, the rain, the snow, the butterflies, the flowers, the deserts. The list could go on and on.

Each aspect of Mother Earth has its own wisdom. Each aspect has its own Soul Language, its own soul song and its own soul dance. When you do soul communication, you can connect with any or all of them. These are just some examples to give you an idea of the possibilities. You can connect with species that are now extinct, like the dinosaurs. You can do soul communication with species that will come into existence in the future.

Using soul communication with Mother Earth is great wisdom. She has seen and experienced almost every human possibility. When you do soul communication with Mother Earth, you can ask specifically to receive wisdom teachings from her present incarnation. It is not the only one that Mother Earth has had. Since it is the one that most people are familiar with, it will give you the most useful teachings. However, you can also ask Mother Earth to teach you wisdom from her other incarnations.

It is no accident that we refer to this planet that is our home as Mother. You can ask why through soul communication. You probably have an immediate answer from logical thinking. That answer would be accurate and true, but there is much more wisdom that

Mother Earth can give. She will be happy to do soul communication with you. Think of your communications with your own mother. Those are often special moments. You remember those special moments as great treasures. They influence your life in a profound way. This is true when you do soul communication with Mother Earth. It will be a special and unique connection with her. What she shares will be deep and profound. It will be a treasure for you.

Doing soul-to-soul communication with Mother Earth is great service. It is service to Mother Earth. It is service to you and all humanity. At this time, Mother Earth is very fragile. Many aspects of this planet are in great danger. There are species in the animal world, the plant world and the insect world that are in danger. There are many who are concerned about Mother Earth. Ordinary people, scientists and many politicians realize her health is very fragile. There are conferences, projects and many other efforts to improve her health. At this point, most of these are gatherings at which people analyze the situation. They develop plans and strategies to improve the situation. All of this is very good. We honor and respect it. It is not enough.

To truly help Mother Earth return to good health, it is absolutely necessary to speak to her soul. Ask her directly what is needed. When you speak to Mother Earth, she will respond with great compassion and care. She will teach you secrets that you would find difficult to imagine. She will teach you ways to help her return to health. If you are concerned about a particular area, then speak to that area. Many in the United States are still concerned about the impact that Hurricane Katrina has been having on New Orleans. Many feel great sadness and a sense of paralysis surrounding that event. If the action plans were done after speaking with the soul of Katrina and the soul of New Orleans, the possibility of beneficial change would increase, and the changes would occur much faster. Conventional planning strategies can be accelerated ten, twenty, thirty and even a hundred times. That would bring action. It would bring healing.

Through soul communication, the action and healing would be exactly what are needed. What is truly needed and what is planned logically do not always match. Logical planning relies on limited information. When the soul provides solutions, the limits are removed. Logical planning is usually based on precedents that have been successful. In contrast, creativity is a hallmark of soul communication. Often the suggestions would not be thought of in days, months or even years.

Asking the soul of New Orleans what is needed makes sense logically also. If you want to find out what is most important to a person, it is best to speak directly to the person. If you want to know what a person's greatest need is on a physical level, it is best to ask the person. This is true for the soul of New Orleans also. This is obvious but it has not become part of the public approach to solving problems. That is quite all right. We are only at the beginning of the Soul Light Era. Even if the planners and decision-makers do not use this approach, we can use it. We can ask the soul of New Orleans what we can do to help. This will be very different from what the government can do. It will be on a smaller scale in the physical realm, but it will be quite significant, because we can do much on the level of the soul.

Soul communication can be used with Mother Earth in countless other ways. For example, you can do soul communication with any of the historical periods of Mother Earth. You can do soul communication with any of the cultures on Mother Earth. This is a particularly important type of soul communication to use at the present time because many cultures are in conflict with one another. Many cultures do not appreciate or respect other cultures.

When you do soul communication with the cultures on Mother Earth, there are many possibilities. One of the best questions to start with is, "What is your message for me today?" Another excellent question is, "What is the wisdom you have to teach?" You can ask these two questions over and over again. When you first ask the questions, the answer will be superficial. The soul of the culture is trying to find out what you will do with the information. Why are you asking? Very few people have asked the soul of any culture for its wisdom, its teachings and its message.

When you ask, at first it will be surprised. I will give you a secret for receiving great information immediately. Use my name. You can start by saying, "Master Sha suggested that I ask you for a teaching by sharing your wisdom." You can say, "Master Sha wants you to give me a message today." If you are wondering whether or not this will make a difference, try asking your question both ways. First, just say, "Dear soul of _____ culture, what is your message?" The next day, use my name. Compare the responses you receive. After using my name several times, the soul of the culture will realize it is important to give you profound teachings and wisdom. You will not need to continue to use my name. You will have established a soul-to-soul connection.

Another question to ask the soul of a culture is, "How can cultures live in harmony?" This is a key question. As soon as you ask, you might hear a response. Continue with further soul communication. You will receive more details and greater wisdom. The soul of the culture might also give you practices to help create harmony between cultures. Asking how cultures can live in harmony is great service. However, now is not the time in the history of Mother Earth for harmony to be a universal reality. Mother Earth needs to experience purification. Do not interfere with the process. Whatever teaching you receive on bringing about harmony, you may use it for a local situation. Do not use it nationally or globally. You may use it for your town or city. If you try to bring harmony on a national or global scale, you will likely hurt your soul journey, because at this time you do not have enough virtue to effect national or global transformation. When you do have more virtue, then you can bring healing to larger groups. Until then, be respectful of the Soul World and your soul standing and use the information only on a local level. Even the ability to do this much is amazing. It changes the quality of light in your entire town. It changes the quality of light for the culture.

Doing soul communication with the culture will give you much information. It will also be service for the culture. If you are a part of that culture, the information and teachings will be very helpful in understanding your approaches and your attachments. It is somewhat similar to receiving soul communication from your past. This is another example of how soul communication can be used for Mother Earth.

Mother Earth's physical condition is very prominent in many people's awareness. There is a huge amount of pollution on Mother Earth. There have been countless meetings, plans, projects, regulations and laws addressing this. Some of these approaches have had great success. Overall, however, success has been very limited. Conventional approaches to pollution usually involve analyzing the situation and creating strategies to address existing problems. Typically, a great deal of information and statistics is gathered. Plans are developed based on an analysis of all of these data. Most of these plans depend on huge funding from governments. Very often, this is where the plans are blocked. Meanwhile, Mother Earth's situation continues to worsen.

The conventional approaches have left Mother Earth in a very sad condition. On the occasions when these approaches have had some success, the work and the funding have usually come from private groups or other groups not directly dependent on money from government sources. These successes have been limited.

One particular aspect of pollution that is creating great difficulties for many countries and cities is the amount of garbage that we human beings generate. Landfills have reached maximum capacity

in many areas. Consequently, the only choice appears to be trans-
porting the excess waste to other areas. This is a solution, but it is
only a stopgap, not a real solution. The excess waste is being moved
to another part of Mother Earth, but the conditions that create the
excess in the original area are still there. The root cause is still there.
There is a huge amount of energy and karma connected with the
landfill and the garbage that it receives. What this "solution" does is
transfer excess energy and karma to another area. This is not a good
idea. To transfer excess energy to another area that also cannot use
it is not a good idea. This is true for one's physical body. It is every
bit as true for the body of Mother Earth.

When excess energy is transferred from one part of Mother Earth
to another and the energy remains stagnant, the adverse impact on
Mother Earth's health is huge. When excesses are transferred over
and over, the impact grows. What can be done to solve this situation? By now, I hope that your automatic response is: *Do soul communication!* Speak to the soul of the landfill. Speak to the soul of the
excess waste. Speak to the soul of those who generate the garbage.
Speak to the soul of the areas that are receiving the excess. Every
one of these souls will have profound wisdom to share with you.

The situation with garbage is only one of the many situations
present on Mother Earth which can give you profound teachings.
You can ask for these teachings from any areas of concern. Mother
Earth has many places where there is a need for healing. At this
time, we cannot try to bring healing to all of them. Simply speak to
the souls of those places that touch your heart the most. Learn their
wisdom. At the appropriate time, healing will be given. In the mean-
time, send your unconditional love and unconditional forgiveness.

Let us join hands together now to offer service to Mother Earth
to assist her on her spiritual journey, to help her purify and uplift
her soul. Say: *Dear soul, mind and body of Mother Earth, I love you. Thank
you for nurturing my life. I am deeply appreciative and honored. Thank you.*

Thank you. Thank you. Dear soul, mind and body of unconditional love and unconditional forgiveness, I love you. Can you please offer a blessing to Mother Earth? I cannot thank you enough. Thank you. Thank you. Thank you.

Then chant *unconditional love, unconditional love, unconditional love, unconditional love, unconditional forgiveness, unconditional forgiveness, unconditional forgiveness, unconditional forgiveness.* You can chant repeatedly for three minutes or for as long as you can. Visualize Mother Earth receiving divine golden, rainbow, purple or crystal light. Visualize her purifying and healing. Each time you chant the mantras *unconditional love* and *unconditional forgiveness,* you are offering service to Mother Earth to bless her spiritual journey. In return, she will offer her love and forgiveness to you, for she is also a servant.

This is the time to learn. This is the time to receive the wisdom and the teaching, to learn the practices and the most appropriate ways to bring healing. Learning the wisdom from all of the difficult situations on Mother Earth is extremely important. Connecting with the soul of each situation is important. It is great service to do this.

It is our privilege at this time in the history of Mother Earth to receive the most profound secrets. Throughout the centuries, a limited number of people have received some information, but it was never complete. What was received was appropriate for the old era. However, we are in a new era. In this era, many things will be revealed that have been secret heretofore. An example is teachings from the numerous sacred sites on Mother Earth. You can learn profound wisdom by speaking to the soul of each of these places. Each of these souls has its own teachings, wisdom, healings, blessings and practices. They are needed at this time. They will help in the purification of Mother Earth. They will help as the Soul Light Era continues. They can be revealed now because they are on the deepest soul level. In the previous era when the mind was in charge, it was not possible to access these teachings. Even if people had heard the teachings, they would not have understood them.

It is a wonderful opportunity and privilege to be able to receive all of these treasures at this time. Mother Earth has many things to share with humanity. When we learn what she wants to share through soul communication, we are assisting in the transformation of the consciousness of humanity and beyond. Mother Earth is in many ways the best teacher for those who dwell upon her. Humanity has come from Mother Earth and is part of Mother Earth. Our physical makeup in many ways matches the physical makeup of our beloved planet. Therefore, humanity will harmonize with her teachings in a special way.

In particular, the sacred teachings from the sacred sites will bring about a new frequency and vibration. Humanity will use the teachings immediately. Humanity will integrate these frequencies and vibrations at an accelerated pace. Using soul communication to receive these teachings is a huge service. No one person will receive the complete and total teaching. Many people will need to do soul communication with each sacred site. Together, we will have a more complete idea. This will allow the souls of the sacred sites to connect with many different souls. Each connection will reveal a particular aspect of the wisdom. Each soul communication will connect at its particular frequency and vibration. Putting it all together will give information and teachings helpful to a wide variety of people and in many different circumstances.

The soul of each sacred site has a special place in Jiu Tian. When you communicate with these souls, you are making a special connection with Jiu Tian. This benefits every level of your being. It benefits all humanity and beyond. It is another example of how to use soul communication with Mother Earth. Continue to find and apply more ways to communicate with Mother Earth. Use your imagination, listen to your soul and follow the suggestions. Soul communication with Mother Earth is a wonderful gift. It is profound service. It is a blessing and a privilege to offer this service.

Soul communication is one of the most important tools we are given by the Divine at this time in the Soul Light Era, which is a special time in the history of Mother Earth. Use this tool with great respect and gratitude. The wonderful thing is that the more we use it, the better it becomes. It brings great joy and delight to the Divine to bless us because we are using soul communication. It is a special gift from the Divine to assist us at this time.

Notes

[22] The two highest-level saints in charge of the Akashic Records are Yan Wang Ye and Jin Fa Sheng Shi ("Golden Hair Saint Servant").

Conclusion

In this book you have received teachings on what soul communication is and why it is important. You have learned about its significance and benefits. You have received teachings and practices on how to open your soul communication channels. The teachings carry blessings. Read this book several times. It is as powerful as attending a live workshop or listening to teleclasses with me.

If you are having difficulty opening one or another of your soul communication channels, read the relevant section many times. Ask the soul of that section to bless you. Always do this with no attachment and no expectation. When you have an expectation or attachment, you are anxious and stressed. This will very effectively block the flow of light. Releasing expectations and attachments will allow the light to flow. It will allow everything to vibrate. You will get results much faster. Keep in mind that the work is yours, but the results belong to God. This awareness will help you to relax.

Perhaps you think you have released expectations and attachments, yet your soul communication channels are still not opening. Remember my teachings on testing and purification. Whatever does or does not take place is a gift. Say "thank you" when your Third Eye opens widely. Say "thank you" when it continues to rest. This is true for every one of the soul communication channels.

You have a wonderful opportunity to learn soul communication. If you already can do soul communication, you can improve. This book will assist you. When you do soul communication, it is with the Divine and the highest saints. There is always the possibility of receiving more. None of us can say, "I have complete information from the Divine and the highest saints." There will always be more.

This book assists you in connecting with deeper wisdom and more profound teachings.

You have received information on how soul communication helps your soul journey. I have given you many practical suggestions on how to use this treasure for healing, teaching and service. All of these suggestions are completely practical. Anyone can follow these suggestions at any time, anywhere, with any situation. The more often you follow these suggestions, the more your ability will grow. Use these teachings throughout the day and your day will become a continuous flow of soul communication. This is a most precious treasure.

The suggestions I have made will only be significant if you use them. Practice what I have taught. Use these suggestions throughout your day. The transformation you will experience will be amazing. When your day becomes a flow of soul communication, you are living "in the condition." You are living in the condition of being connected with the Divine and the highest saints. It is an honor and privilege beyond words. It is priceless. Living in the condition of soul communication will heal, bless, rejuvenate and transform every aspect of your being.

It has been my honor and privilege to present these teachings to you.

Thank you. Thank you. Thank you.

A Divine Download Gift

Dear Reader,

Heaven's Library and Master Sha are delighted to offer you a priceless permanent divine healing and blessing treasure as a gift from the heart of the Divine.

This divine download is named *Zhi Gang Sha Soul Rainbow Light Ball and Soul Rainbow Liquid Spring for Divine Lower Dan Tian.* It is a subdivided divine soul which carries divine love, light and frequency of all the colors of the rainbow. The light ball brings you the blessings of the yang aspect of the Divine. The liquid spring brings you the blessings of the yin aspect. Once this divine soul is transmitted or downloaded to your soul, it will remain with your soul forever.

As soon as you receive *Zhi Gang Sha Soul Rainbow Light Ball and Soul Rainbow Liquid Spring for Divine Lower Dan Tian,* you can invoke it to build your Lower Dan Tian, boosting your energy, vitality, stamina and immunity, grounding and balancing your emotions, and improving your mental clarity. As you have learned, a powerful Lower Dan Tian supports not only your soul communication channels, but every aspect of your being. You can also share the profound benefits of this divine download to serve others.

To receive this permanent divine gift and to learn more, visit www.heavenslibrary.com.

Thank you. Thank you. Thank you.

Acknowledgments

I am honored to present this volume in Heaven's Library's Soul Wisdom Series to you. I could not have given you this teaching, wisdom, knowledge and practice without the guidance, support and blessing of many souls.

I first thank my most beloved teacher and adoptive father, Master Zhi Chen Guo. He has trained me for fifteen years. He has tested me. He has blessed me. He has opened his heart and soul to me. Without his teachings, his training and his blessings, I could not have written this book. I cannot thank my most beloved spiritual father enough.

I am deeply grateful to the Divine. As a divine channel, vehicle and servant, I am honored to be able to receive and transmit the divine wisdom, knowledge and practice in this book and all the books of Heaven's Library to selected divine writers. Without the greatest honor, teaching and blessing from the Divine, I could not have written this book. I cannot thank the Divine enough.

I thank all my spiritual fathers and mothers in Heaven, including my first Shi Fu, Yun Zhong Zi and beloved Shi Jia Mo Ni Fuo. There are countless others, too many to name. Without their teachings, guidance and blessings, I could not have written this book. I cannot thank them enough.

I thank all the divine writers, divine editors, members of my business team and students who are serving humanity, Mother Earth and the Divine with me. Without their support and blessing, I could not have written this book.

I thank all my other physical teachers in this lifetime. I have been honored to study with many great masters in many areas of wisdom, knowledge and practice. Without their teachings, wisdom and blessings, I could not have written this book.

I give special thanks to my beloved family, my dear parents and grandparents, my beloved wife and children, my adored sisters and brother. Without their love, understanding and support, I could not have given you this book.

I thank you, dear reader, for opening your heart and soul to receive the teaching, wisdom, knowledge and practice in this book. May this book serve you and many others well.

I thank every soul in the universe. Let us join hands, hearts and souls in love, peace and harmony to create a peaceful and harmonized Mother Earth and universe.

Thank you. Thank you. Thank you.

Master Zhi Gang Sha

Dr. Sha's Teachings and Services

Books:

Power Healing: The Four Keys to Energizing Your Body, Mind & Spirit (HarperSanFrancisco, 2002)

Soul Mind Body Medicine: A Complete Soul Healing System for Optimum Health and Vitality (New World Library, 2006)

Living Divine Relationships (Heaven's Library, 2006)

Body Space Medicine by Dr. Zhi Chen Guo (Foreword by Dr. Sha) (Heaven's Library, 2007)

Soul Wisdom I (Heaven's Library, 2007)

Healing Service:

Free Remote Healing Teleconference, Tuesdays, 5:30–6:30 p.m. Pacific Time. Register one time at www.drsha.com for this regular weekly healing service.

CDs and DVDs:

The Voice of the Universe: Power Healing Music (Qi Records, 2002). Four powerful universal mantras recorded by Dr. Sha:

- *God's Light*
- *Universal Light*
- *Shining Soul Light*
- *Follow Nature's Way*

Available as individual CDs.

The Music of Soul Dance (Golden Light Media, 2007). A ten-CD boxed set of Heaven's music to inspire and guide your Soul Dance.

Power Healing to Self-Heal Ten Common Conditions (Institute of Soul Mind Body Medicine, 2004). On this DVD, Dr. Sha teaches the Four Power Techniques® to self-heal:

- Anxiety
- Back pain
- Carpal tunnel syndrome
- Common cold
- Constipation
- Energy booster
- Headache
- Knee pain
- Menopause
- Weight loss

He also offers personal blessings for each condition.

Power Healing with Master Zhi Gang Sha: Learn Four Power Techniques to Heal Yourself (Institute of Soul Mind Body Medicine, 2006).

This four-DVD set offers a comprehensive teaching of the wisdom, knowledge and practice of Power Healing and Soul Mind Body Medicine. All aspects of Body Power, Sound Power, Mind Power and Soul Power are covered in depth. Dr. Sha reveals and explains many secret teachings and leads you in practice.

www.drsha.com

Heal the soul first; then healing of the mind and body will follow.

— *Zhi Gang Sha*

www.heavenslibrary.com
1.888.339.6815